Lifting the Mists

A Simple Guide to a Complex Welfare System

For elderly immigrants and their families

Malti Patel

Mr. Majmundar published a book on algebra-factorization for secondary students in 1998. In 2001, Mr. H. N. Varma an Indian supreme court lawyer wrote a biography of Mr. Majmundar, entitled "An Exalted Indo-American," published by the great Indian publishers, New Delhi India. Mr. Majmundar wrote and published a book on welfare, *Mapping the Maze*, in 2003. It was subsequently translated into Gujarati and Marathi. Mr. Majmundar has written many articles on welfare, published in India and in America. He also wrote a column for *India Post* a weekly magazine published in Northern California.

Malti Patel
Texas
November 2007

Foreword

By Harikrishna Majmundar
Author of *Mapping the Maze.*

A thorough review of welfare programs in America is long overdue. The welfare reform bill was due for review in 2002, but it has been postponed every year since.

The welfare reform bill, officially titled the Personal Responsibility and Work Opportunity Reconciliation Act of 1996, ended a sixty-year-old tradition of entitlement to public assistance for the poorest of Americans. It put time limits on benefits, tied aid closely to work, and transferred authority for setting benefits and administering programs from the federal to the state level. What is more, the bill greatly reduced or eliminated the eligibility of legal immigrants and the disabled for such programs.

The devolution of authority to the states has in fact left wide powers to local caseworkers, with no provision for reviewing the workers' performance by an independent authority. This is the saddest part of the story.

The 1996 legislation signaled the victory of three great forces: the war on dependence, the devolution of public authority, and the application of market models to public policy. The importance assigned to work cannot be questioned. America is great because of hard work done by one and all. However equating work with monetary compensation devalues precisely those activities most critically needed in communities: caring, learning, worshipping, associating, socializing and helping. It seems bizarre to me that such a rich society would entrust such important tasks independent body. Discrimination is not intended but is practiced widely. This should be put an end to.

- Require welfare claimants and recipients to be treated with compassion and dignity.

- Do not use ignorance of the rules to reduce or deny the legitimate claims of those in need.

This helpful and informational book by Malti Patel will go a long way to make welfare claimants and recipients more knowledgeable about the complicated welfare rules. Malti is an intelligent, hardworking, focused and determined individual whose abilities are complemented by commitment to her religious beliefs and practice, as well as her social work, especially with elders in need. She has really come to the forefront by assisting many senior citizens to realize their legal rights pertaining to Social Security and medical benefits. Her services are truly altruistic and an asset to the community at large.

I wish her well as she continues her excellent work of educating those in need, and hope to see her publish many more such books in due course.

Palo Alto
November 2007

Preface

As Marcia K. Meyers of the University of Washington has observed, "The first form of help that low-income individuals need is information. Learning about the benefits for which they may be eligible turns out to be a surprisingly difficult hurdle for many. Much information generally available is both inaccurate and inadequate. Although low-income individuals are often portrayed as knowledgeable and savvy consumers of welfare services, more systematic research reveals that their information is often both limited and inaccurate." This book attempts to remedy that situation and assist those in need.

Silent features of American Welfare System and its effect on society

Books on welfare in America are written in so many forms and in such minute detail that one more book might seem to be a superfluity. However the thorny maze of public assistance programs and regulations needs to be cleared every now and then.

Private assistance to the needy and disabled in America is given, this much is clear, with great reluctance. Americans are under a great misconception that to offer private assistance to a needy person is to rob him of the opportunity to improve himself by his own efforts. Many in America genuinely believe that one does harm to the person in the long run if he helps him in the short run. The history of private assistance in this country from the time the Puritans arrived to this present day also informs the philosophy of public assistance:

1. Those who do not work shall not eat.

2. Those who need public assistance should not be refused, and those who do not need should not be given.

3. The quantum of public assistance should always be less than what one can earn by full time work at minimum wages – The principle of less eligibility.

4. Welfare depends upon residency.

5. Public assistance is a matter of last resort. The claimant must exhaust all his or her means and only when there is no other way to survive may he or she apply for assistance.

6. It should be made clear to the claimant that public assistance is meant for survival only and not to lift him or her from poverty. People should make their own efforts to avoid poverty.

After the American Civil War, the country began to turn towards the social Darwinism of Herbert Spencer—the survival of the fittest. However America also had a charitable impulse and tradition that were too strong to be eliminated completely. Welfare survived, but in a lukewarm fashion.

The idea that financial distress was a moral failing and thus should not be relieved especially through public assistance became even stronger in the late 19th century. In the 21st century these ideas have been incorporated in the laws governing welfare.

Many immigrants who are welfare claimants or recipients have both resources and income outside the USA. They nurture false hopes that those who dispense public assistance are not likely to find out about them. A Chinese proverbs says "If you do not want any body to know it, Do not do it." The truth will come out sooner or later, with heavy penalties to those who have been benefited by concealment.

The safest way to get public assistance and to retain it is to get rid of any attribute that makes one ineligible for it. The website www.ssa.gov provides detailed instructions for obtaining and retaining public assistance, covering all cases. This book contains those instructions in simple and easy-to-understand question answer format. It is advisable to scrupulously follow social security requirements.

Only the well-informed are blessed!

Malti Patel
Texas
November 2007

Table of Contents

Part 1   Questions 1

General Benefits Questions 2
Retirement Benefits Questions 5
Survivor Benefits Questions 10
Spousal Benefits Questions 15
Medicare 19
Medicare Questions 21
Medicaid 33
How To Apply for Medicare Savings Programs 36
Understanding How to Get Disability or SSI Benefits. 37
Increase Your Odds of Winning 38
Disability Questions 40
PRUCOL Questions 49
Supplemental Social Security Questions 54
Computation of Benefits 66
Check Payment Direct-Deposit Questions 69
Earnings and Employment Questions 72
Self Employment Questions 75
Forms and Publications Questions 81
International Questions 83
Laws and Regulations Questions 89

Part 2 Information from POMS 93

The Program Operations Manual System (POMS) 94
Eligibility for Hospital Insurance (HI) HI 00801.131: 95
Enrollment and coverage periods (HI 00801.133): 97
Joint Bank Account 99
Temporary Absence From the State 101
Establishing Absence and Presence in the U.S. (RS 02610.020): 102
Payment to Aliens living outside USA 104
ALIENS Non-Payment Exemptions (GN 01701.150) 106
Gifts (SI 00830.520) 107
Gifts of Travel Tickets (SI 00830.521): 109
Over Payments Waiver (GN 02250.001) 111
Treatment of Assets Under Income and Resources Rules. 112
Qualifying Quarters (QQs) 114
"Similar Fault" Definition 117
Federal Means Tested Benefits 121
Public Charge 121
Disadvantaged by Bad or Delayed SS Department Advice 123
Acronyms 124
Appendix: Donate life: Become an Organ and Tissue Donor 125

xi

Part 1
Questions

This part of the book is divided into various categories of questions with answers that may help you resolve your issues or provide you with needed information.

General Benefits Questions

Q. What is SSI?

A. SSI, or Supplemental Security Income, is a federal program that provides monthly cash payments to people in need. SSI is for people who are 65 or older, as well as for blind or disabled people of any age, including children.

There were many piecemeal benefits plans for old and disabled people. In 1974, the US Government combined all the plans and came up with one single plan called Supplemental Security Income (SSI).

Those who do not get enough social security (low wage earners) are given supplemental income up to the maintenance level when they retire. Incidentally, those who have not worked or earned enough credits to qualify for social security but who receive social security because of disability are also given supplemental income up to the maintenance level.

To qualify for SSI one also must have little or no income and limited resources.

Effective January 2007 the SSI payment for an eligible individual is $623 per month and $934 per month for an eligible couple.

Every year the SSI benefit amount is adjusted for inflation.

Generally, to be eligible for SSI, an individual also must be a resident of the United States and must be a citizen or a noncitizen lawfully admitted for permanent residence or have worked 40 quarters.

You must live in the United States or the Northern Mariana Islands to get SSI. If you are not a U.S. citizen, but you are a resident, you still may be able to get SSI. For more information, ask for a copy of "Supplemental Security Income (SSI) For Noncitizens " (Publication No. 05-11051).

For more information, read booklet, "Understanding SSI" on web site, http://www.socialsecurity.gov/notices/supplemental-security-income/text-understanding-ssi.html

Q. I am 65 years old and I have worked for 40 quarters. I am getting social security. And also get SSI. Why my SSI amount is less than SSI amount given to the person who has never worked. Is this fair?

A. Total amount given to both are same. You get social security amount first and balance from SSI as Supplemental Income up to the maintenance level. Person who has not worked gets full amount as supplemental income only.

You have advantage of getting social security amount, even if you are absent from USA. While person who has not worked does not get anything once he leaves USA for more than 30 days.

Q. When I start receiving benefits, will my benefit amount be the same for the rest of my life?

A. Your benefit amount will not stay the same. Generally, the benefit amount increases each year and protects beneficiaries against inflation. SSA provides an annual cost-of-living increase that is based on the

General Benefits Questions

consumer price index. The 2007 increase for beneficiaries is 3.3 percent and the 2006 increase was 4.1 percent. There is another way that your benefit might increase. When you work, you pay Social Security taxes. And because you pay these taxes, Social Security Department refigures your benefits to take into account your extra earnings. If the worker's earnings for the year are higher than the earnings that were used in the original benefit computation, Social Security substitutes the new year of earnings. The higher your earnings, the more your refigured benefit might be.

Q. Can I borrow from my future Social Security benefits?

A. No. The Social Security program is not intended to be a source from which people can borrow.

Q. My mother is disabled and I need to stay home to help care for her. Does Social Security provide benefits to a caregiver or housekeeper?

A. You may enquire with your Welfare department to determine if there are any locally sponsored programs that might provide you with assistance.

Retirement Benefits Questions

Q. What is a "representative payee"?

A. A representative payee is the person, agency, organization, or institution selected to receive and manage benefits on behalf of an incapable beneficiary. This includes a parent who is receiving benefits on behalf of his/her minor child. Some beneficiaries are not able to manage or direct the management of their finances because of their youth or mental or physical impairment.

For such people, Congress provided for payment to be made through a representative payee who receives and manages benefit payments of the beneficiary. When a representative payee is appointed, the SSA field office provides the payee with complete information about the use of benefits; i.e., proper disbursement and how benefits should be conserved or invested and ensures that the payee understands the fiduciary nature of the relationship, that benefits belong to the beneficiary and are not the property of the payee. The payee is informed about the penalties for using the benefits other than for the benefit of the beneficiary and that an annual accounting is required.

Q. How are my retirement benefits calculated? Are my retirement benefits figured on my last five years of earnings?

A. Social Security benefits are based on earnings averaged over most of a worker's lifetime. Your actual earnings are first adjusted or "indexed" to account for changes in average wages since the year the earnings were

Retirement Benefits Questions

received. Then SSA calculates your average monthly indexed earnings during the 35 years in which you earned the most. Apply a formula to these earnings and arrive at your basic benefit, or "primary insurance amount" (PIA). This is the amount you would receive at your full retirement age, for most people, age 65. However, beginning with people born in 1938 or later, that age will gradually increase until it reaches 67 for people born after 1959. For more information, see "The Full Retirement Age is increasing" on this web site, http://www.socialsecurity.gov/pubs/ageincrease.htm

As you can see from the above, the benefit computation is complex and there are no simple tables that will tell you how much you will receive.

Q. What are credits and how do I earn them?

A. Credits are based on the amount of your earnings. You can earn up to a maximum of 4 credits each year when you work in a job or operate your own business as a self-employed person and pay Social Security taxes.

Each year the amount of earnings needed for credits goes up slightly as average earnings levels increase. In 2007, you earn one credit for each $1,000 of your earnings. So if you have earned at least $4,000 during the year, you get the maximum 4 credits. In 2006, the amount for one credit was $970.

The credits you earn remain on your Social Security record even if you change jobs or have no earnings for a while. Your work history determines your eligibility for retirement or disability benefits or your family's eligibility for survivor's benefits when you die.

Retirement Benefits Questions

Q. How long does a person need to work to become eligible for retirement benefits?

A. Everyone born in 1929 or later needs 40 Social Security credits to be eligible for retirement benefits. You can earn up to four credits per year, so you will need at least 10 years to become eligible for retirement benefits.

During your working years, earnings covered by social security are posted to your Social Security record, and you earn credits based on those earnings.

Each year the amount of earnings needed for a credit rises as average earnings levels rise. In 2006, you receive one credit for each $970 of earnings, up to the maximum of four credits per year. For 2007, you receive one credit for each $1,000 of earnings.

Q. My husband and I are both entitled to our own Social Security benefits. Will our combined benefits be reduced because we are married?

A. No. When each person of a married couple works in employment covered under Social Security and they meet all other eligibility requirements to receive Social Security benefits, their lifetime earnings are calculated independently to determine their Social Security benefit amount. Therefore, each spouse receives a monthly benefit amount based on his or her own earnings. Couples are not penalized simply because they are married.

Q. Can I opt out of Social Security? Can I withdraw taxes that I have paid for Social Security coverage?

A. No. Social Security coverage is mandatory. But consider this, unlike your private plan, Social Security provides disability and survivors coverage in addition to retirement benefits. And Social Security generally offers greater protection for family members than private pensions.

The law also does not permit a refund of Social Security taxes.

Q. I paid the maximum amount of Social Security taxes for many years and retired early. Then I took part-time employment and I am now earning much less. How will this affect my benefit at age 62 and at full retirement age?

A. First, if you begin receiving Social Security benefits at age 62, the earliest possible age for receiving retirement benefits, your benefit amount will be lower than if you had waited until full retirement age. Second, because of the years when you worked part-time and had low earnings, your benefit amount may be lower than if you had continued in your previous job paying the maximum. Your benefit payment is based on how much you earned during your working career. Higher lifetime earnings result in higher benefits.

For more information, call Social Security at the toll-free number, 1-800-772-1213 from 7 a.m. to 7 p.m., Monday through Friday, to ask for "Your Retirement Benefits: How it is Figured (Publication No. 05-10070).

Q. How are benefits computed if I have less than 35 years of work?

A. Social Security Administration uses the highest 35 years of earnings to compute an individual's benefit amount. If the individual does not have 35 years of earnings, they will use all of the earnings on the record, and they add $0.00 earnings for each of the remaining years (to make the total up to 35 years) before computing the benefit amount.

Survivor Benefits Questions

Q. What are the requirements for a survivor to receive Social Security benefits?

A. In order to receive survivor's benefits, the deceased worker must have earned the required number of Social Security credits and survivors must meet the following requirements:

- A widow or widower may be able to receive full benefits at age 65 if born before 1940. (The age to receive full benefits is gradually increasing to age 67 for widows and widowers born in 1940 or later.) Reduced widow or widower benefits can be received as early as age 60. If the surviving spouse is disabled, benefits can begin as early as age 50.

- A widow or widower can receive benefits at any age if she or he takes care of the deceased worker's child who is entitled to a child's benefit and is younger than age 16 or disabled.

- A deceased worker's unmarried children who are younger than age 18 (or up to age 19 if they are attending elementary or secondary school full time) also can receive benefits. Children can get benefits at any age if they were disabled before age 22 and remain disabled. Under certain circumstances, benefits also can be paid to stepchildren, grandchildren or adopted children.

- A deceased worker's dependent parents can receive benefits if they are age 62 or older. (For parents to qualify as dependents, the deceased worker would have had to provide at least one-half of their support.)

- A deceased worker's former wife or husband who is age 60 or older (as early as age 50 if disabled) can get benefits if the marriage lasted at least 10 years. A former spouse, however, does not have to meet the age or length-of-marriage rule if he or she is caring for his/her child who is younger than age 16 or who is disabled and also entitled based on the deceased worker's work. The child must be the deceased worker's former spouse's natural or legally adopted child.

Q. How long must you be married to a spouse to collect benefits when the spouse dies?

A. Generally, a person can qualify for widow's or widower's benefits if he or she was married to the deceased worker for at least nine months just before the worker died. However, you do not need to be married to the worker for any specific length of time if:

- You are the biological parent of the worker's biological child;
- You legally adopted the worker's child while you were married to him or her and before the child attained age 18;
- You are the parent of a child who was legally adopted by the worker while you and the worker were married and before the child attained age 18;
- You and the worker were married and both of you legally adopted a child under age 18;
- You were entitled or potentially entitled to spouse's, widow(er)'s, mother/father's, or parent's benefits, or to childhood disability benefits in the month before the month you married the deceased worker;

Survivor Benefits Questions

- You were entitled or potentially entitled to a widow(er)'s, child's (age 18 or over) or parent's insurance annuity under the Railroad Retirement Act (RRA) in the month before you married the deceased worker;

- The worker was married previously to an institutionalized spouse, but was not allowed to divorce him or her under State law. After the spouse died, he or she married you within 60 days;

- You were married to the worker at the time his or her death and you had been married to and divorced from him or her before and the previous marriage lasted 9 months;

- The worker's death occurred in the line of duty while he or she was a member of a uniformed service serving on active duty; or

- The worker's death was accidental. (Note: The worker's death is considered "accidental" only if he or she received bodily injuries through violent, external and accidental means and, as a direct result of the bodily injuries and independent of all other causes, died within 3 months after the day he or she received the injuries.)

- If the worker could not reasonably have been expected to live for nine months at the time you married him or her, then you cannot qualify for benefits under the last three conditions.

Q. How much is a working widow allowed to earn without losing any Social Security widow's benefits?

A. The law that determines what happens when you work and get benefits at the same time was changed, effective January 2000. This change in law applies to widow(er)s as well as retired workers. While you're working, your benefit amount will be reduced only until you reach your full retirement age. Full retirement age for earnings test purposes is currently age 65 and 8 months for persons born 1/2/41 through 1/1/42.

SSA will use this formula to determine how much your benefit must be reduced:

If you are under full retirement age when you start getting your Social Security payments, $1 in benefits will be deducted for each $2 you earn above the annual limit. For 2007 that limit is $12,960; for 2006, it is $12,480.

In the year you reach your full retirement age $1 in benefits will be deducted for each $3 you earn above a different limit. In that year, SSA only count earnings before the month you reach your full benefit retirement age. For 2007, this other limit is $34,440; for 2006, it is $33,420.

Starting with the month you reach full retirement age you will get your benefits with NO limit on your earnings.

Please Note: Earned income is defined as income from wages or net earnings from self-employment. Pensions, 401K distributions, dividends, interest, and IRA distributions are NOT earned income.

Q. What are the requirements for receiving disabled widow's benefits?

A. You may be able to get disabled widow(er)'s benefits at age 50 if you are found to meet Social Security's disability requirement. Your disabling impairment must have started before age 60 and within 7 years of the latest of the following dates:

The month the worker died; OR the last month you were entitled to mother's or father's benefits on the worker's record; OR the month your previous entitlement to disabled widow(er)'s benefits ended because your disability ended.

Survivor Benefits Questions

Q. Am I entitled to widow's or widower's benefits if I remarry?

A. Generally, you cannot get widow's or widower's benefits if you remarry before age 60. But remarriage after age 60 (or age 50 if you are disabled) will not prevent you from getting benefit payments based on your former spouse's work. And at age 62 or older, you may get benefits based on your new spouse's work, if those benefits would be higher.

Spousal Benefits Questions

Q. Can I receive reduced retirement benefits at age 62 under my record then at full retirement age receive full spouse's benefits?

A. If you choose to receive a reduced benefit before full retirement age on your own record, you are not entitled to the full spouse's benefit rate upon reaching full retirement age, and a reduced benefit rate is payable for as long as you remain entitled to spouse's benefits.

When you apply for reduced retirement benefits, SSA will check to see if you are eligible for both your own retirement benefits and for benefits as a spouse. If you are eligible for both, you will get your own benefits first. If you are due additional benefits, you will get a combination of benefits equaling the higher spouse's benefit. If you are not eligible for both because your spouse is not yet entitled, but you are due a higher amount when he or she starts receiving Social Security benefits, then the higher spouse's benefit is payable to you when your spouse applies for retirement benefits. Remember, you cannot receive spouse's benefits until your spouse files for retirement.

Q. My wife doesn't have enough work to qualify for Social Security or Medicare. Can she qualify on my record?

A. The question you've raised applies to husbands as well as wives. Even if he or she has never worked under Social Security, your spouse at full retirement age can receive a benefit equal to one-half of your full

Spousal Benefits Questions

retirement amount. (If your spouse will receive a pension for work not covered by Social Security such as government foreign employment, the amount of his or her Social Security benefits on your record may be reduced.)

Your spouse can begin collecting the benefits as early as age 62, but the amount will be permanently reduced by a percentage based on the number of months up to his or her full retirement age. Your spouse who is caring for your child who is also receiving benefits can receive the full one-half benefit amount no matter what his or her age is. Your spouse would receive these benefits until the child reaches age 16. At that time, the child's benefits continue, but your spouse's benefits stop unless he or she is old enough to receive retirement benefits (age 62 or older) or survivor benefits as a widow or widower (age 60).

Q. What are the benefit amounts a husband or wife may be entitled to receive?

A. A spouse receives one-half of the retired worker's full benefit unless the spouse begins collecting benefits before full retirement age. In that case, the amount of the spouse's benefit is permanently reduced by a percentage based on the number of months before he/she reaches full retirement age.

For example, based on the full retirement age of 65, if a spouse begins collecting benefits:

- At 64, the benefit amount would be about 46 percent of the retired worker's full benefit.
- At age 63, it would be about 42 percent, and
- At age 62, 37.5 percent.

However, if a spouse is taking care of a child who is either under age 16 or disabled and receiving Social Security benefits, a spouse gets full (one-half) benefits, regardless of age.

If you are eligible for both your own retirement benefit and for benefits as a spouse, SSA always pay your own benefit first. If your benefit as a spouse is higher than your retirement benefit, you'll receive a combination of benefits equaling the higher spouse's benefit.

Q. Can my spouse collect benefits at age 62 from her work and earnings and then receive a combined total up to 50 per cent from my account when I start receiving benefits at age my full retirement age?

A. Your spouse can start receiving reduced retirement benefits on her own record at age 62. If the amount she receives on her own record is less than what she would be entitled to as a spouse, she would receive a higher spouse's benefit when you start receiving benefits. However, because she began receiving Social Security before reaching full retirement age, she will receive a reduced benefit rate that is less than the full 50 percent amount for as long as she remains entitled to spouse's benefits.

When your spouse applies for reduced retirement benefits, SSA will check to see if she is eligible for both her own retirement benefits and for benefits as a spouse. If she is eligible for both, SSA will pay her own benefits first. If she is due additional benefits, she will get a combination of benefits equaling the higher spouse's benefit. If she is not eligible for both because you are not yet entitled, but is due a higher amount when you start receiving Social Security benefits, then the higher spouse's benefit is payable to her when you apply for retirement benefits. Remember, she cannot receive spouse's benefits until you file for retirement.

Spousal Benefits Questions

Q. I have never worked but my spouse has. What will my benefits be?

A. You can be entitled to as much as one-half of your spouse's benefit amount when you reach full retirement age. If you want to get Social Security retirement benefits before you reach full retirement age, the amount of your benefit is reduced permanently. The amount of reduction depends on when you will reach full retirement age.
For example:

- If your full retirement age is 65, you can get 37.5 percent of your spouse's unreduced benefit at age 62.

- If your full retirement age is 66, you can get 35 percent of your spouse's unreduced benefit at age 62.

- If your full retirement age is 67, you can get 32.5 percent of your spouse's unreduced benefit at age 62.

The amount of your benefit increases at later ages up to the maximum of 50 percent at full retirement age. If your full retirement age is other than those shown here, the amount of your benefit will fall between 32.5 percent and 37 percent at age 62.

However, if you are taking care of a child who is under age 16 or who gets Social Security disability benefits, you get full benefits, regardless of age. Your spouse must file for benefits before you can begin receiving them on his or her record.

Q. If a spouse collects one-half of her husbands benefit does that reduce the husbands benefit by one-half?

A. No. The receipt of spouse's benefits by a husband or wife does not reduce the benefit of the primary wage earner.

Medicare

What Is Medicare?

Medicare is America's health insurance program for people age 65 or older. Certain people younger than age 65 can qualify for Medicare, too, including those who have disabilities and those who have permanent kidney failure or amyotrophic lateral sclerosis (Lou Gehrig's disease). The program helps with the cost of health care, but it does not cover all medical expenses or the cost of most long-term care.

Medicare Has Four Parts

1. Hospital insurance (Part A):

Medicare Part A helps pay for inpatient care in a hospital or skilled nursing facility (following a hospital stay), some home health care and hospice care.

2. Medical insurance (Part B):

Medicare Part-B helps pay for doctors' services and many other medical services and supplies that are not covered by hospital insurance.

3. Medicare Advantage (Part C):

Medicare Part-C plans are available in many areas. People with Medicare Parts A and B can choose to receive all of their health care services through one of these provider organizations under Part C.

4. Prescription drug coverage (Part D):

Medicare Part D helps pay for medications doctors prescribe for treatment.

You can get more detailed information about what Medicare covers from Medicare & You (Publication No. CMS-10050). To get a copy, call the Medicare toll-free number, 1-800-MEDICARE (1-800-633-4227), or go to www.medicare.gov. If you are deaf or hard of hearing, you may call TTY 1-877-486-2048.

Medicare Questions

Q. Who can get Medicare Hospital insurance (Part A)?

A. Most people age 65 or older who are citizens or permanent residents of the United States are eligible for free Medicare hospital insurance (Part A).

You are eligible at age 65 if:

- You receive or are eligible to receive Social Security benefits; or
- You or your spouse (living or deceased, including divorced spouses) worked long enough in a government job where Medicare taxes were paid; or
- You are the dependent parent of someone who worked long enough in a government job where Medicare taxes were paid.

If you do not meet these requirements, you may be able to get Medicare hospital insurance by paying a monthly premium. Usually, you can sign up for this hospital insurance only during designated enrollment periods.

Q. When should I apply for Medicare?

A. If you are already getting Social Security retirement or disability benefits or railroad retirement checks, you will be contacted a few months before you become eligible for Medicare and given the information you need. You will be enrolled in Medicare Parts A and B automatically. However, because you must pay a premium for Part B coverage, you have the option of turning it down.

If you are not already getting retirement benefits, you should contact SSA department about three months before your 65th birthday to sign up for Medicare. You can sign up for Medicare even if you do not plan to retire at age 65. Once you are enrolled in Medicare, you will receive a red, white and blue Medicare card showing whether you have Part A, Part B or both. Keep your card in a safe place so you will have it when you need it.

You will also receive a Medicare & You (Publication No. CMS-10050) handbook that describes your Medicare benefits and Medicare plan choices.

Q. What are Special enrollment situations?

A. You also should contact Social Security about applying for Medicare if:

- You are a disabled widow or widower between age 50 and age 65, but have not applied for disability benefits because you are already getting another kind of Social Security benefit.
- You are a government employee and became disabled before age 65;
- You, your spouse or your dependent child has permanent kidney failure;
- You had Medicare medical insurance in the past but dropped the coverage; or
- You turned down Medicare medical insurance when you became entitled to hospital insurance (Part A).

Medicare Questions

Q. What is the Initial enrollment period for Part B?

A. When you first become eligible for hospital insurance (Part A), you have a seven-month period (your initial enrollment period) in which to sign up for medical insurance (Part B). A delay on your part will cause a delay in coverage and result in higher premiums. If you are eligible at age 65, your initial enrollment period begins three months before your 65th birthday, includes the month you turn age 65 and ends three months after that birthday. If you are eligible for Medicare based on disability or permanent kidney failure, your initial enrollment period depends on the date your disability or treatment began.

Q. When does my enrollment in Part B become effective?

A. If you accept the automatic enrollment in Medicare Part B, or if you enroll in Medicare Part B during the first three months of your initial enrollment period, your medical insurance protection will start with the month you are first eligible. If you enroll during the last four months, your protection will start from one to three months after you enroll.

The following chart shows when your Medicare Part B becomes effective:

If you enroll in this month of your initial enrollment period:	Then your Part B Medicare coverage starts:
1	The month you become eligible for Medicare
2	The month you become eligible for Medicare
3	The month you become eligible for Medicare
4	One month after enrollment

Medicare Questions

If you enroll in this month of your initial enrollment period:	Then your Part B Medicare coverage starts:
5	Two months after enrollment
6	Three months after enrollment
7	Three months after enrollment

Q. What is the General enrollment period for Part B.

A. If you do not enroll in Medicare Part B during your initial enrollment period, you have another chance each year to sign up during a "general enrollment period" from January 1 through March 31. Your coverage begins the following July.

However, your monthly premium increases 10 percent for each 12-month period you were eligible for, but did not enroll in, Medicare Part B.

Q. What is the Special enrollment period for people covered under an employer group health plan?

A. This section explains the Special enrollment period for people covered under an employer group health plan.

If you are 65 or older and are covered under a group health plan, either from your own or your spouse's current employment, you have a "special enrollment period" in which to sign up for Medicare Part B.

This means that you may delay enrolling in Medicare Part B without having to wait for a general enrollment period and paying the 10 percent premium surcharge for late enrollment.

The rules allow you to enroll in Medicare Part B any time while you are covered under the group health plan based on current employment; or enroll in Medicare Part B during the eight-month period that begins with the month your group health coverage ends, or the month employment end, whichever comes first.

Special enrollment period rules do not apply if employment or employer-provided group health plan coverage ends during your initial enrollment period.

If you do not enroll by the end of the eight-month period, you will have to wait until the next general enrollment period, which begins January 1 of the next year. You also may have to pay a higher premium, as described in publication "General enrollment period for Part B".

Note: Even though the full retirement age is no longer 65, you should sign up for Medicare three months before your 65th birthday.

Q. Who can apply for Medicare insurance (Part B)?

A. Anyone who is eligible for free Medicare hospital insurance (Part A) can enroll in Medicare medical insurance (Part B) by paying a monthly premium. Some beneficiaries with higher incomes will pay a higher monthly Part B premium. For more information, see "Medicare Part B Premiums: New Rules for Beneficiaries with higher Incomes (Publication No. 05-10161).

If you are not eligible for free hospital insurance (Part-A), you can buy Medicare insurance (Part-B), without having to buy hospital insurance if:

- You are age 65 or older and;
- You are a U.S. citizen;
- Or a lawfully admitted noncitizen who has lived in the U.S. for at least five years.

Medicare Questions

Q. What are Medicare Advantage plans (Part C)?

A. If you have Medicare Parts A and B, you can join a Medicare Advantage plan. With one of these plans, you do not need a Medigap policy, because Medicare Advantage plans generally cover many of the same benefits that a Medigap policy would cover.

Q. What are Medicare prescription drug plans (Part D) and what is the enrollment period for (Part D)?

A. Anyone who has Medicare hospital insurance (Part A), medical insurance (Part B) or a Medicare Advantage plan (Part C) is eligible for prescription drug coverage (Part D). Joining a Medicare prescription drug plan is voluntary, and you pay an additional monthly premium for the coverage. You can wait to enroll in a Medicare Part D plan if you have other prescription drug coverage but, if you don't have prescription coverage that is, on average, at least as good as Medicare prescription drug coverage, you will pay a penalty if you wait to join later. You will have to pay this penalty for as long as you have Medicare prescription drug coverage.

Enrollment period (Part D):

People who become newly entitled to Medicare should enroll during their initial enrollment period (January 1st to March 31st). After the initial enrollment periods, the annual coordinated election period to enroll or make provider changes will be November 15 – December 31 each year. There also will be special enrollment periods for some situations.

Q. What help low-income people get for Medicare premiums payment?

A. If you cannot afford to pay your Medicare premiums and other medical costs, you may be able to get help from your state. States offer programs for people who are entitled to Medicare and have low income. The programs may pay some or all of Medicare's premiums and also may pay Medicare deductibles and coinsurance. To qualify, you must have Part A (hospital insurance), a limited income, and, in most states, your resources, such as bank accounts, stocks and bonds, must not be more than $4,000 for a single person or $6,000 for a couple.

You can go online to get more information about these programs from the Centers for Medicare & Medicaid Services (CMS) web site. Visit www.medicare.gov and find Publication No. CMS-10126. If you need help paying Medicare costs, there are programs that can help you save money.

Only your state can decide if you qualify for help under these programs. To find out, contact your state or local medical assistance (Medicaid) agency, social services or welfare office.

You also may be able to get extra help paying for the annual deductibles, monthly premiums and prescription co-payments related to the Medicare prescription drug program (Part D). You may qualify for extra help if you have limited income (tied to the federal poverty level) and limited resources.

If you have both Medicaid with prescription drug coverage and Medicare, Medicare and Supplemental Security Income, or if your state pays for your Medicare premiums, you automatically will get this extra help and you don't need to apply.

Note: SSI recipients do not have to apply for extra help.

Medicare Questions

Q. I no longer need Medicare Part B, because I am covered by other health insurance. How do I disenroll from Medicare Part B?

A. If you wish to disenroll from Medicare Part B, you will need to submit form CMS-1763 to the Social Security Administration. The form is used to voluntarily terminate entitlement to Supplementary Medical Insurance (Part B) and Premium hospital Insurance and is owned by the Center for Medicare and Medicaid Services (CMS).

CMS requires that a personal interview be conducted with every individual who wishes to terminate entitlement and so they do not offer form CMS-1763 on the public Internet site. The form will be completed during an in-person or phone interview so that they can ensure that the beneficiary understands the ramifications of termination.

After the interview, Social Security Administration representative is required to provide you with a letter outlining the consequences of voluntary termination and of the right to withdraw the termination request before coverage ends. Disenrolling is a serious decision; if you wish to reenroll later, you may have to pay a surcharge.

Q. I get both SSI and Medical/Medicaid, I have received a premium due notice for Medicare Part-A and Part-B premiums. What should I do?

A. To resolve this, All SSI recipients are advised to apply for QMB (Qualified Medicare Beneficiary) first and also give reply to the premium due notice indicating that you are not liable to pay premiums as you are covered under QMB/SSI/Medicaid.

For more information on how other health insurance plans work with Medicare call the Medicare toll-free number 1-800-MEDICARE (1-800-633-4227).

Q. I am 65 and my wife is 62 and receiving spouse's benefits. When does she qualify for Medicare benefits?

A. Most people must wait until age 65 to qualify for Medicare benefits. Some people can get Medicare at any age. This includes people who:

- Have been getting Social Security disability benefits for 24 months;
- Have kidney failure and require dialysis;
- Have had a kidney transplant; or
- Receive disability benefits because they suffer from amyotrophic lateral sclerosis (also known as Lou Gehrig's disease).

Q. Will a one-time increase in my income (for example, due to property sales or capital gains) affect my Part B premium forever?

A. No. Each year SSA request your most recent tax return information from the Internal Revenue Service (IRS). To determine the 2007 Part B premium, IRS generally provides information for tax year 2005. For 2008, IRS will generally provide information for tax year 2006. They use your modified adjusted gross income (MAGI) to determine your premium for one year. Your MAGI is a combination of your adjusted gross income and tax exempt interest income.

Your tax return for 2006 will reflect only your income for that year. So, if your premium increased in 2007 due to a one-time increase in your income in 2005, such as sale of property, it could decrease in 2008. Your 2008 Part B premium depends on your income for tax year 2006.

Medicare Questions

Q. Can I appeal the amount of my Medicare Part B premium?

A. If you disagree with the decision regarding your Medicare Part B premium amount, you have the right to appeal. You can request an appeal in writing by completing a "Request for Reconsideration " (Form SSA-561-U2). You can find the appeal form online at www.socialsecurity.gov/online/ssa-561.html or request a copy through toll-free number 1-800-772-1213 (TTY 1-800-325-0778), or you can contact your local Social Security office to file your appeal. You do not need to file an appeal if any of the following applies to you.

You can request a new decision and ask that they use more recent tax information if:

- They used 2004 tax data to determine your 2007 premium and you have a signed copy of your 2005 tax return; or

- One of the following happened and the change will make a difference in the income level they consider:

    - You married;

    - You divorced or your marriage was annulled;

    - You became a widow or widower;

    - You or your spouse stopped working or reduced work hours;

    - You or your spouse lost income from income-producing property due to a disaster or other event beyond your control; or

    - Your or your spouse's benefits from an insured pension plan stopped or were reduced.

Once you show evidence of the event and provide proof or an estimate of your reduced income, SSA will update your records and correct your Part B premiums back to the earliest time in the year you had Part B.

You also can request a new decision and ask that they use more accurate tax return information if:

* You amended your tax return for the year they used to determine your premium and it changes the income.
* You provide proof from IRS of an error in the tax return information.
* Your tax filing status for the year they used to determine your premium was "married filing separately" and you did not live with your spouse at any time during that year.

To report the change, you can use Form SSA-44 "Medicare Part B Income-Related Premium-Life-Changing event" or call toll-free at 1-800-772-1213 (TTY 1-800-325-0778) or visit your local Social Security office.

Q. I get only Medicare benefits based on my 40 quarters of earnings. Do I have to inform the state about my travel out side USA?

A. Yes, you should inform the State about your travel. A person with only Medicare benefits pays their own Medicare-B premium, which is automatically deducted from the retirement benefits check every month. If that person goes out of the country without informing the state, the state continues to pay the Medicare premium (that is, continues to deduct the premium from the retirement benefits check) even though the person cannot use Medicare benefits while abroad. To avoid this scenario, it is important to inform the state about travel out of the country and request the state to stop Medicare coverage for the period you are out of the country.

Medicare Questions

On return to the USA, write a letter informing the state of your return, and requesting the state to restart Medicare immediately from the date you arrive. (For those who pay their own premium, Medicare starts on the day they return to the USA).

Q. Does a spouse, age 62 receive Medicare benefits when his/her aged 65 husband/wife does?

A. Generally not. The minimum age for Medicare eligibility is 65. But, if you've been getting Social Security disability benefits for 24 months you can receive Medicare at any age

Q. If I retire at age 62 will I be eligible for Medicare at that time?

A. No. Medicare benefits based on retirement do not begin until a person is age 65. If you retire at age 62, you may be able to continue to have medical insurance coverage through your employer or purchase it from a private insurance company until you turn age 65 and become eligible for Medicare.

Medicaid

What Is Medicaid?

Medicaid is a medical assistance program that is partially funded by the Federal Government but run by each State. Medicaid pays for basic medical care for people and families with low incomes and resources. People who are blind or disabled, age 65 or older, children, or members of families with dependent children may be eligible. Using broad Federal guidelines, each State runs its own Medicaid program. The State decides who is eligible and the amount of medical care and services it will cover.

Representatives in your local public assistance office can tell you about eligibility for Medicaid and whether you qualify. You may also want to ask them about other assistance in your community for which you may be eligible. For more information on the Medicaid program, see website http://www.cms.hhs.gov/home/medicaid/asp.

There are several Medicare Savings Programs that help people with low Income and Resources levels pay for health care coverage. You must meet certain Income and Resources limits to qualify for these programs.

The Resources (Assets) limits are the same for all programs. Your personal assets (cash, money in the bank, stocks, bonds, etc.) cannot exceed $4,000 for an individual or $6,000 for married couples. Exclusions include a home, household goods and personal belongings, one car, a life insurance policy up to a cash value of $1,500 per person, a prepaid burial plan (unlimited if irrevocable; up to $1,500 if revocable),

Medicaid

and a burial plot. For six months after receipt, retroactive Social Security or SSI benefits are also excluded. The value of these items is not calculated into your personal asset limit.

Medicare Savings Programs

Qualified Medicare Beneficiary (QMB):

The Qualified Medicare Beneficiary (QMB) program helps people whose assets are not low enough to qualify them for Medi-Cal/Medicaid.

For QMB, your monthly income cannot exceed $851 if you are single. If married, a couple's monthly income cannot exceed $1,141. (Note: these figures change in April every year)

QMB pays for the following:

- Medicare Part A premium for those who do not receive it automatically because they are not eligible for Social Security. (The premium is $226 or $410 per month in 2007, depending on the number of Social Security quarters earned.)
- Standard Medicare Part B premium ($93.50 per month in 2007).
- Deductibles for both Part A and Part B. The Part A (hospital inpatient) deductible is $992 per benefit period (2007). The Part B annual deductible is $131 in 2007.
- Co-insurance under both Parts A and B.

For example, under Part A, QMB would pay the $992 first-day hospital deductible, the $248 per day for hospital days 61-90, and the $496 per day (in 2007) for the 60 hospital reserve days. Part B Medicare coverage pays 80% of physician and outpatient expenses, and QMB would pay the remaining 20% co-insurance, as long as the person sees doctors and other providers that accept Medi-Cal.

Note: Most people do not have to pay a Medicare Part A premium. But if you are not entitled to receive Medicare Part A for free, you may benefit the most from the QMB program because QMB pays this premium, which is $410 per month in 2007. (Medi-Cal does not pay the Part A premium).

Specified Low-income Medicare Beneficiary (SLMB):

The Specified Low-income Medicare Beneficiary (SLMB) program helps low-income persons by paying their Medicare Part B premiums ($93.50 per month in 2007). These premiums would otherwise be deducted from their Social Security checks.

For SLMB, your monthly income cannot exceed $1,021 if you are single. If married, a couple's monthly income cannot exceed $1,369. (Note: these figures changes in April every year.)

Qualified Individual (QI):

The Qualified Individual (QI) program helps low-income people by paying their Part B premiums ($93.50 per month in 2007).

For QI, your monthly income cannot exceed $1,149 ($13,783.50 per year) if you are single. If married, a couple's monthly income cannot exceed $1,541. (Note: these figures changes in April every year.)

How To Apply for Medicare Savings Programs

If you think you qualify under any of the Medicare Savings Program categories, you can apply for help with your Medicare costs.

To enroll in QMB, SLMB, QI you must also be eligible to receive Medicare Parts A and B. If you are already on Medicare, contact your county Department of Social Services to apply for QMB, SLMB, and QI benefits. Applications for the Medicare Savings Programs are processed through the county offices.

If you are not on Medicare, apply at any Social Security office and state in writing that you are applying for conditional Medicare under one of the Medicare Savings Programs. Once you become eligible for Medicare, you should follow up with your county's Department of Social Services to apply for QMB, SLMB, and QI benefits or to verify your application status.

The rules for these programs can be complicated. If you need help, contact your local Health Insurance Counseling and Advocacy Program (HICAP) at (800) 434-0222.

Understanding How to Get Disability or SSI Benefits.

1. Initial application — Every claim for disability and SSI benefits begins with the initial application. 75% of all applicants are denied at this step. SSA looks for a reason to deny benefits. The decision is based on forms you completed and medical records, and your income and resources. You won't meet with anyone involved in making the decision. It is surprising when anyone wins at this step. Don't quit--You must appeal a denial within 60 days.

2. Reconsideration — The second step in the system but the results are worse. 82% of all applicants are denied at this level. SSA reviews your file again and issues a denial; unfortunately it may take months to receive. At this step, only 50% of the original applicants are still in the system, the rest gave up. Appeal the denial immediately. Up to this point in the system you have been a social security number and a file.

3. Request for Hearing before Administrative Law Judge — Congratulations! You have persevered in the system and now have a good chance to win benefits. 53% of all claimants win at this stage.— Why? Primarily because your claim is entitled to be reviewed by a Judge who knows the law and does not work for SSA. Also, you get to testify before the Judge about your inability to work and she/he assesses your credibility. Finally, hopefully you have obtained opinions from your doctors about your inability to work or determine your Income and Resources. You must win your case at the hearing stage; if you do not, you can appeal but your claim will be tied up perhaps for years with the likelihood of success dramatically reduced.

Increase Your Odds of Winning

Now that you have an understanding of how the system works, here are some tips on how you can maximize your chance for success.

1. Appeal every Denial — It bears repeating; DO NOT QUIT after receiving a denial. Now you understand you must get to a hearing. Up to that point SSA and the odds are overwhelmingly against you. Receiving a denial may be cause to celebrate because you are a step closer to a hearing.

2. Retain a Disability Attorney — In case of Disability, retaining an attorney who specializes in disability law should substantially increase your odds of winning. Most claimants have no idea what they need to prove to win their case. Practically all disability attorneys work on a contingency fee. You only pay a fee if you win your case. Also, Federal law sets the maximum amount the fee can be in your case. An attorney will develop your case by obtaining the necessary medical and vocational records and opinions from your doctors that are critical in proving disability.

3. Complete the Social Security Forms — You will complete a dizzying array of forms requesting all sorts of information. Be honest and very brief when completing forms. You won't win your case with the information you give on the forms but you could lose it.

4. Involve your Treating Physician — Your treating physician is critical to success in case of disability. Judges give a treating physician's opinion regarding a patients' disability tremendous weight. If your physician is not sympathetic to your claim you may want to make a change to one who is.

The purpose of this section is to convey hope that you can win your case and obtain benefits with perseverance and knowledge of the system.

Please do not give up . . . appeal and pray

Disability Questions

Q. How does Social Security decide if I am disabled?

A. Disability under Social Security for an adult is based on your inability to work because of a medical condition. To be considered disabled:

- You must be unable to do work you did before and they decide that you cannot adjust to other work because of a medical condition.

- Your disability must last or be expected to last for at least one year or to result in death.

For more information, read the publication, Disability Benefits (SSA Publication No. 05-10029) on website http://www.socialsecurity.gov/pubs/10029.html

Q. I am receiving Social Security disability benefits. Will my benefits be affected if I work and earn money?

A. There is special rule called "work incentives" that help you keep your cash benefits and Medicare while you test your ability to work. For example, there is a trial work period during which you can receive full benefits regardless of how much you earn, as long as you report your work activity and continue to have a disabling impairment.

The trial work period continues until you accumulate nine months (not necessarily consecutive) in which you perform what is called "services" within a rolling 60-month period. SSA considers your work to be "services" if you earn more than $640 a month in 2007. For 2006, this amount was $620. After the trial work period ends, your benefits will stop for months your earnings are at a level they consider "substantial," currently $900 in 2007. For 2006, this amount was $860. Different amounts apply to people who are disabled because of blindness.

For an additional 36 months after completing the trial work period, you can get your benefits again if your earnings fall below the "substantial" level and you continue to have a disabling impairment.

Q. What is the difference between Social Security disability and SSI disability?

A. The Social Security Administration is responsible for two major programs that provide benefits based on disability: Social Security Disability Insurance (SSDI), which is based on prior work under Social Security, and Supplemental Security Income (SSI). Under SSI, payments are made on the basis of financial need.

Social Security Disability Insurance (SSDI) is financed with Social Security taxes paid by workers, employers, and self-employed persons. To be eligible for a Social Security benefit, the worker must earn sufficient credits based on taxable work to be "insured" for Social Security purposes. Disability benefits are payable to blind or disabled workers, widow(er)s, or adults disabled since childhood, who are otherwise eligible. The amount of the monthly disability benefit is based on the Social Security earnings record of the insured worker.

Supplemental Security Income (SSI) is a program financed through general revenues. SSI disability benefits are payable to adults or children who are disabled or blind, have limited income and resources, meet the living arrangement requirements, and are otherwise eligible. The monthly payment varies up to the maximum federal benefit rate, which

Disability Questions

may be supplemented by the State or decreased by countable income and resources.

Q. Can I receive Social Security benefits and SSI?

A. You may be able to receive SSI in addition to monthly Social Security benefits, if your Social Security benefit is low enough to qualify.

The amount of your SSI benefit depends on where you live. The basic SSI check is the same nationwide. Effective January 2007, the SSI payment for an eligible individual is $623 per month and $934 per month for an eligible couple. However, many states add money to the basic check.

Following is a list of some States that supplement the basic SSI amount.

- California
- Hawaii
- Massachusetts
- New Jersey
- New York
- Pennsylvania
- Rhode Island
- Vermont
- Washington D.C.

If you get SSI, you also may be able to get other help from your state or county. For example, you may be able to get Medicaid, food stamps, or

Disability Questions

some other social services. For information about all the services available in your community, call your local social services department or public welfare office.

For more information, you should read Social Security pamphlet " Supplemental Security Income" on website http://www.socialsecurity.gov/pubs/11000.html

You should call toll-free number, 1-800-772-1213, to find out if you might be eligible for SSI in your state.

Q. Is there a time limit on Social Security disability benefits?

A. No. Your disability benefits will continue as long as your medical condition has not improved and you cannot work. Your case will be reviewed at regular intervals to make sure you are still disabled. If you are still receiving disability benefits when you reach full retirement age, it will automatically be converted to retirement benefits.

Q. Why there is a five-month waiting period for Social Security disability benefits?

A. The five month waiting period ensures that during the early months of disability, SSA does not pay benefits to persons who do not have long-term disabilities. Social Security disability benefits can be paid only after you have been disabled continuously through out a period of five full calendar months. Therefore, Social Security disability benefits will be paid for the sixth full month after the date your disability began.

43

Disability Questions

Q. I currently receive Social Security disability benefits. My disabilities have worsened and I have other health problems. Can my monthly benefit amount be increased?

A. No. Your Social Security disability benefit is based on the amount of your lifetime earnings before your disability began and not the degree or severity of your disability.

Q. What is the earliest age that I can receive Disability benefits?

A. There is no minimum age as long as you meet the very strict social security definition of disability. But to qualify for disability benefits you must have worked long and recently enough under Social Security to earn the required number of work credits. You can earn up to a maximum of four work credits each year. The amount of earnings required for a credit increases each year as general wage levels rise. The number of work credits you need for disability benefits depends on your age when you become disabled. Go to http://www.socialsecurity.gov/dibplan/dqualify3.htm to see how many credits you may need to qualify for disability benefits.

Q. How do workers' compensation payments affect my disability benefits?

A. Disability payment you receive from workers' compensation and/or another public disability payment may reduce you and your family's Social Security benefits.

Your Social Security disability benefit will be reduced so that the combined amount of the Social Security benefit you and your family receive plus your workers' compensation payment and/or public disability payment does not exceed 80 percent of your average current

Disability Questions

earnings. (Note that the unreduced benefit amount is counted for income tax purposes.)

Workers' compensation payment is one that is made to a worker because of a job-related injury or illness. It may be paid by federal or state workers' compensation agencies, employers, or insurance companies on behalf of employers.

Public disability benefit (PDB) payments that may affect your Social Security benefit are those paid under a federal, state, or local government law or plan. A PDB is not usually based on a work-related disability. They differ from workers' compensation because the disability that the worker has may not be job-related. Examples are civil service disability benefits, military disability benefits, state temporary disability benefits, and state or local government retirement benefits which are based on disability.

Q. How many credits are required to be eligible for disability?

A. The number of work credits you need to qualify for disability benefits depends on your age when you become disabled. Also, the credits must have been earned within a certain time period. Generally, you need 20 credits earned in the last 10 years, ending with the year you become disabled.

Younger workers may qualify with fewer credits. For example, a worker who becomes disabled before age 24 needs to have earned six credits in the three-year period ending when disability starts.

A worker who becomes disabled between age 24 to age 31 needs to have credits for half the time between age 21 and the time disability starts. If disability starts at age 27, the worker would need credit for three years of work (12 credits)) out of the past six years between age 21 and age 27.

Disability Questions

For additional information, read publication, "Disability (SSA Publication No.05-10029)" on website
http://www.socialsecurity.gov/pubs/10029.html

Q. I was told Social Security would give Supplemental Security Income to children who were born prematurely. Is this true?

A. Yes, Social Security does provide SSI disability benefits to certain low birth weight infants, whether or not they are premature. A child who weighs less than 1200 grams (about 2 pounds, 10 ounces) at birth can qualify for SSI on the basis of low birth weight, if otherwise eligible. A child who weighs between 1200 and 2000 grams at birth (about 4 pounds 6 ounces) AND who is considered small for his or her gestational age may also qualify. For this second category of low birth weight infants, the following chart shows the gestational age at birth and corresponding birth weight that satisfies "**small for gestational age**" criterion.

Gestational Age (weeks)	Weight at Birth
37-40	Less than 2000 grams (4 lb 6 oz)
36	1875 grams or less (4 lb 2 oz)
35	1700 grams or less (3 lb 12 oz)
34	1500 grams or less (3 lb 5 oz)
33	1325 grams or less (2 lb 15 oz)

Even if a child who was born prematurely does not fall into one of the "low birth weight" categories, he or she may still qualify for SSI if the evidence in his or her record shows that he or she meets the "Definition of disability for children" as per website
http://www.socialsecurity.gov/disability/disability_starter_kits_child_fac

tsheet.htm for another reason. Call 1-800-772-1213 (TTY 1-800-325-0778) or contact your local office for more information.

Q. If my disability benefits end because of my work, will I have to file a new application, if I can't work anymore?

A. If your benefits have ended because of work, you can file a request to start your benefits again without having to file a new application. There are some important conditions as follow to be noted:

You have to be unable to work because of your medical condition.

The medical condition must be the same as or related to the condition you had when they first decided that you should receive disability benefits.

You have to file your request to start your benefits again within 60 months of the date you were last entitled to benefits.

Note:

- Filing Disability claim again in future, one does not require to wait for initial 5 months period again..
- If initially it is determine that disability is not going to be improved soon, it is advisable to get a letter from the doctor indicating that disability improvement will take more than a year. This will help you to get disability earlier and you do not have to wait for one year determination period.

Disability Questions

Q. I applied for Social Security disability benefits and received a letter that says I am medically disabled but SSA will review the non-medical part of my claim. What are non-medical requirements?

A. To receive Social Security Disability benefits a person must meet Social Security's definition of disability and meet certain non-medical eligibility requirements. Examples of non-medical eligibility requirements include proof of age, employment, marital status, or Social Security coverage information.

State agencies (usually called Disability Determination Services or DDSs) make the medical determination on a claim. Local Social Security offices are responsible for verifying non-medical eligibility requirements.

Q. Are there any special services or Social Security information available for people who are blind?

A. There are a number of services and products specifically designed for people who are blind. Many of social security publications are available in Braille, audiocassette tapes, compact disks or in enlarged print for people who are blind or visually impaired. The publication "If You Are Blind or Have Low Vision –How we can Help, and other publications in alternative formats can be obtained by calling toll-free, 1-800-772-1213 (for the deaf or hard of hearing, call TTY number, 1-800-325-0778), Monday through Friday, 7 a.m. to 7 p.m.

PRUCOL Questions

WHAT IS PRUCOL?

There is not a specific definition for an alien who is considered "Permanently residing under color of law" (PRUCOL) in immigration law, as PRUCOL is not a distinct immigration category. PRUCOL status is established when a "non-qualified" alien is permanently or indefinitely residing in the U.S. and USCIS is not taking steps to deport them. Aliens, such as applicants for political asylum or withholding of deportation, who have not yet received a final order, are considered PRUCOL. In most cases, PRUCOL clients can be identified by documentation that shows USCIS knows their whereabouts combined with the absence of documentation indicating deportation is in process.

Examples of PRUCOL aliens are listed below in alphabetical order.

Abused aliens who have self-petitioned under VAWA but not yet received a "Notice of Prima Facie" eligibility, as described in WAC 388-424-0001.

Abused aliens who are a relative of a U.S. citizen with an approved I-130 petition but not meeting the other requirements of battered immigrants, as described in WAC 388-424-0001.

- Applicants for adjustment of status.

- Applicants for asylum.

PRUCOL Questions

- Applicants for cancellation of removal.

- Applicants for suspension of deportation.

- Applicants for withholding of deportation or removal.

- Cancellation of removal granted. (Note: If a person is granted cancellation of removal based on having been abused they are a "qualified alien," not PRUCOL.)

- Deferred action granted. (Note: If a person is granted deferred action based on having an approved self-petition as an abused alien, they are a "qualified alien," not PRUCOL.)

- Deferred enforced departure granted.

- Family Unity granted.

- "K" status granted. "K," "S," "U," or "V" statuses, designated on a person's visa, allow holders to work and eventually to adjust to Lawful Permanent Resident (LPR) status.

- Order of suspension granted.

- Citizens of Palau.

- Paroled into the U.S. for a period of one year or less.

- Residing in the U.S. since prior to January 1, 1972.

- "S" status granted.

- Eligible to petition as special immigrant juveniles. These are juveniles who have been declared a "dependent of the state" and eligible for long-term foster care due to abuse, neglect, or abandonment.

- Stay of deportation granted.

- Stay of removal granted.

- Suspension of deportation granted. (Note: If a person is granted suspension of deportation based on having been abused they are a "qualified alien," not PRUCOL.)

- Temporary protected status granted.

- Voluntary departure granted – definite time.

- Voluntary departure granted – indefinite time.

- "U" status granted.

- "V" status granted.

Q. As a PRUCOL immigrant, what benefits can I receive?

A. You may be eligible for only some federal benefits, including:

Emergency Medicaid, immunizations, testing and treatment of communicable diseases.

Disaster relief, School lunch, child nutrition programs, foster care and adoption assistance, Higher education loans, Head Start and other education programs, Job Training Partnership Act, community programs necessary to protect life or safety such as domestic violence shelters, and the Consolidated Emergency Assistance Program.

In addition, you may be eligible for following state programs:

Cash benefits (Family Assistance Program or General Assistance Unemployable Program) Food stamps (Food Assistance Program) and Medical benefits for pregnant women as well as health care programs for emergency costs. The state health care programs for children and families receiving cash assistance were terminated on October 1, 2002.

For more information see the pamphlet called Washington State Immigrant Health Care Transition: October 2002. You may also be eligible for the Basic Health Plan and Hospital Charity Care.

Q. Can receiving cash benefits prevent me from getting a green card (lawful permanent residence) or becoming a citizen?

A. The INS may deny your green card application if INS finds that you are dependent on cash benefits for support. This is called being a "public charge". Getting cash benefits may make it difficult to get your green card if the following circumstances exist:

The INS applies public charge rules to your category of immigration status, AND

The benefits you are getting are cash benefits, AND

The benefits are the sole support of your family.

Some immigrants with PRUCOL status, such as asylum applicants, do not have to show they are not likely to become a public charge. Consult an immigration attorney for questions or read the brochure "New INS Guidance on "Public Charge" : When Is It Safe to Use Public Benefits" to find out if public charge rules apply to you.

Even if public charge does apply to you and you have received cash benefits, you can show the INS that your need for cash assistance is temporary and will not affect your ability to support yourself or your family in the future. It is o.k. to receive non-cash benefits (like medical care and food stamps) because the INS does not consider these benefits (except for medical benefits for persons institutionalized for long-term care) in determining, if you are a public charge.

However, immigrants who fraudulently receive public assistance may have trouble becoming citizens and may even face deportation if convicted of a crime.

Q. If I am an undocumented immigrant can I get Medical/Medicaid?

A. If you are an undocumented immigrant you cannot get regular medical/Medicaid. However you can get restricted Medical which can cover following:

- Emergencies
- Long-term medical care
- Kidney dialysis
- Care for pregnant woman from the start of pregnancy through 60 days after the child is born.

Supplemental Social Security Questions

Q. What is the difference between Social Security disability and SSI disability?

A. The Social Security Administration is responsible for two major programs that provide benefits based on disability. Social Security Disability Insurance (SSDI), which is based on prior work under Social Security, and Supplemental Security Income (SSI). Under SSI, payments are made on the basis of financial need.

Social Security Disability Insurance (SSDI) is financed with Social Security taxes paid by workers, employers, and self-employed persons. To be eligible for a Social Security benefit, the worker must earn sufficient credits based on taxable work to be "insured" for Social Security purposes. Disability benefits are payable to blind or disabled workers, widow(er)s, or adults disabled since childhood, who are otherwise eligible. The amount of the monthly disability benefit is based on the Social Security earnings record of the insured worker.

Supplemental Security Income (SSI) is a program financed through general revenues. SSI disability benefits are payable to adults or children who are disabled or blind, have limited income and resources, meet the living arrangement requirements, and are otherwise eligible. The monthly payment varies up to the maximum federal benefit rate, which may be supplemented by the State or decreased by countable income and resources.

Q. How much will I receive in SSI benefits?

A. The amount of your benefit depends on where you live. The basic SSI check is the same nationwide. Effective January 2007, the SSI payment for an eligible individual is $623 per month and $934 per month for an eligible couple. For January 2006, the SSI payment for an eligible individual was $603 per month and $904 per month for an eligible couple. However, many states add money to the basic check.

If a state provides a supplement, which Social Security includes in the SSI, check then your application for SSI in that state includes the state supplement. Following is a list of States that supplement the basic SSI amount with a link to more information about that State:

- California
- Hawaii
- Massachusetts
- New Jersey
- New York
- Pennsylvania
- Rhode Island
- Vermont
- Washington D.C.

Other states administers its own supplemental payments then you must apply for the supplement at the state agency.

Note: Only California state gives more state supplement amount.

Supplemental Social Security Questions

If you get SSI, you also may be able to get other help from your state or county. For example, you may be able to get Medicaid, food stamps, or some other social services. For information about all the services available in your community, call your local social services department or public welfare office.

For more information, you should read Social Security pamphlet "Supplemental Security Income".

Every year amount gets adjusted with Inflation.

Q. Can my children receive dependent's benefits because I am on Supplemental Security Income?

A. No. Supplemental Security Income (SSI) benefits are based on the needs of the individual and are only paid to the qualifying person. There are no spouse's, children's or survivors benefits payable.

Q. My dad, who is receiving SSI benefits, will be coming to live with me. Since his SSI check goes directly to the bank, does he have to report the move to Social Security?

A. Yes. An SSI beneficiary must report any change in living arrangements within 10 days after the month the change occurs. If you don't, you could end up receiving an incorrect payment and have to pay it back. Failure to report or filing false reports could result in a fine, imprisonment or both. Also, you need to report your new address to Social Security so that you can continue to receive mail from Social Security when necessary. You can report the change by mail or in person at any Social Security office. Social Security's toll-free number is 1-800-772-1213. People who are deaf or hard of hearing may call toll-free TTY

Supplemental Social Security Questions

number, 1-800-325-0778, between 7 a.m. and 7 p.m. on Monday through Friday.

Q. I have applied for SSI. I am a U.S.A citizen. I have two fixed deposit CDS maturing after 2 years. They were taken in 1992. Currently, I am in huge debt. I am planning to pay my debt after 2 years, when my CDS mature. My total debt is more than maturity value of the CDS. Will I be allowed to retain my CDS and be given SSI?

A. No. Social Security Administration considers fixed deposit and Bank CDS as resources. You may have to cash the CDS and pay your debt bringing your resources to below the prescribed limits to qualify for SSI.

Q. I have an ancestral house at a village in India. As per Indian tradition, it is in my name, as I am the eldest surviving male member. My widowed sister stays in it. Its current market value is $7000. My father gave oral instructions to us before he died, not to sale that house as long as my widowed sister is using it, as she does not have any income or resources to support her. The Social Security Administration does not admit/believe this and insisting me to sell the house and bring the money to U.S.A. Can U.S. Government compel me to sell the sacred house of my forefathers and ask my sister to quit from that house?

A. Please note that once you are on welfare, you are considered as second class citizen. Social Security Administration may compel you to sell the house and bring the proceeds to USA. In order to qualify for SSI you have to bring your resources below the prescribed limits first and than apply for SSI. Social security Administration may exempt the sale

57

Supplemental Social Security Questions

of the house while computing your resources if you can make a good case. Valid reasons to exempt the house include the following:

- It is a Hindu undivided property and you are only a Karta (Manager) of the property and the other owners are not willing to sell the property.

- You can provide proof indicating that the owner's reasonable efforts to sell have been unsuccessful for a period of 9 months.

- The sale of the house will cause hardship to your widowed sister.

Q. I am 57 years old. I have come to U.S.A in 1995. I am suffering from obesity and have to move in the wheel chair even in my own house. I live with my daughter. Recently, my daughter has lost her job and she is in financial difficulties. She wants me to pay for my expenditure, which I cannot pay. She is asking me to go back to India if I cannot pay. I have a house in India, which requires extensive repairs. Is there any way to get some redress?

A. Yes. You may apply for disability SSI/Medicaid. You have every chance for getting SSI/Medicaid based on your severe obesity.

Q. How do I apply for Food Stamps?

A. The Food Stamp program is administered by the Department of Agriculture. For more information on the program see the website http://www.fns.usda.gov/fsp/applicant_recipients/default.htm

Note: Filling food stamp application, please note that only you, your wife, and children under age 18 make up your family. If you live with your married son /daughter's family, your son/daughter and your grand children are not included as members of your family.

Q. How does disposal of resources affect SSI eligibility?

A. To be eligible for SSI a person must have $2,000 or less in countable resources. If the person alleges a transfer of resources, it must determine whether the resource transfer was valid. If the transfer was not valid, they may still count the resource toward the $2,000 limit. If the transfer was valid, the resource would no longer be counted toward the $2,000 limit.

Transfers of resources may occur through any of the following types of transactions:

- Sale of property.
- Trade or exchange, one property for another.
- Giving away cash, property or bank accounts, etc.

Since 12/14/99, giving away a resource or transferring it for less than it is worth can make a person ineligible for SSI for up to 36 months. The number of months of ineligibility depends on the value of the resource that was transferred or given away and the compensation, if any, that the individual received for that resource. For more information, please read material on "transfers of resources" in the booklet "Understanding SSI."

Q. Can I leave the country for 2 weeks and still get SSI? I'm going to visit relatives in Mexico for two weeks this summer. Can I still get SSI payments while I'm there?

A. Your SSI usually will stop if you leave the United States for a full calendar month or 30 consecutive days or more. Since you are going to be away for only two weeks, your SSI should not be affected. However,

Supplemental Social Security Questions

it's important that you tell Social Security the date you plan to leave and the date you are planning to come back. Then they can let you know if your SSI will be affected.

Caution: If air ticket is purchased by your child as a gift for your Non-Domestic travel, SSA considers airfare amount towards your income for the month you travel overseas. Because of this reason your resources may exceed SSI limits ($2000 for single and $4000 for married). This may disqualify you for getting SSI. SSI may deduct any payment made to you while were out of the country for less than 30 days.

Suggestions to resolve the above situation:

1. Never borrow cash from your children or relatives for buying air tickets. Borrowing money is considered as income for SSI eligibility. If you do not use the money you borrowed in the same month, it will become resource in the next month.

2. Ask your children to buy an airplane ticket for you with their credit card. In case you decide not to travel or cancel the air ticket, the refund goes back to your children's credit card account and your income is not increased simply by cancellation of an airplane ticket.

Q. Is the SSI payment for an eligible couple twice that of an eligible individual? And if it isn't, why not?

A. The SSI program provides a basic Federal payment for an eligible individual and a larger amount for an eligible couple. The payment for a couple is lower than that made to two individuals because married people living together generally share expenses and live more economically than two people living independently.

Supplemental Social Security Questions

Q. I and my spouse both live in the same state together. We both get SSI benefits. If one of us go to visit my daughter/son, who lives in different state will our SSI benefits be affected?

A. No. If only one spouse travel from one state to another state SSI payment for both should be continued in the original state. If your spouse intend to stay in another state for more than 90 days, you must inform SSA in writing.

Q. I receive SSI payment by checks, directly deposited to my bank. Must I still notify Social Security that I have moved to a new address?

A. Yes. Social security Office needs your correct mailing address to send you notices and other correspondence about your benefits even if you receive your checks directly deposited to your bank.

You can change your address online by answering a series of questions that have to match their records. You can also change your address on the Internet if you have established a permanent password. If you would like to get a password, you can apply online or you can call at 1-800-772-1213. A change of address also may be reported to local Field Offices.

Q. Husband and wife are lawful permanent resident and each has worked for 5 years (Earned 20 qualified quarters credit). Can they apply for SSI?

A. Yes, Each spouse can get credit for work done by other spouse. If both meet 40 qualifying quarters requirement they can apply for SSI.

Supplemental Social Security Questions

Q. One spouse has worked for 10 years and earned 40 qualifying quarters. His non-working spouse entered USA on August 23rd 1996. Can the non-working spouse apply for SSI?

A. The non working spouse who entered USA after 22nd August 1996 has to wait for 5 years to become a qualified Alien (till August 23rd 2001) to use working spouse's credits for applying for SSI benefits.

Q. What is the "family maximum?" My husband died and I applied for Social Security survivor's benefits for my two children and myself. When the Social Security representative took my claim she mentioned something about a "family maximum." I don't fully understand what she meant by the family maximum. Would you please explain this to me?

A. The benefit amount you and your children receive is based on your deceased husband's earnings. The more he paid into Social Security, the greater your benefits will be. However, there is a limit to the amount of money that can be paid each month to a family. The limit is normally referred to as the "family maximum." This limit varies, but it is generally between 150 and 180 percent of the deceased's benefit amount. If the sum of the benefits payable to you and your children is greater than this limit, each of you will receive a benefit amount that is proportionately reduced.

Supplemental Social Security Questions

Q. Is the family maximum adjusted when one child is no longer eligible? I have four children who receive benefits on my account. When one of my children graduates from high school, is the total amount that they receive reduced or is that amount now divided by three instead of four?

A. There is a limit on the amount of benefits that can be paid each month on a person's earnings record. The purpose of this ceiling is to assure that a family will not get considerably more in benefits after a worker retires, becomes disabled, or dies than the family had in earnings when the worker was employed.

When benefits for a family would otherwise exceed the maximum amount payable, the benefits for all members, except the worker, are reduced proportionately to bring the total within the limit. As one child (auxiliary) turns age 18 and is no longer in a secondary school (high school), benefits to the other children will usually increase up to the family maximum. However, the remaining children on the record are each only entitled to no more than 50% of the number holder's benefit, and that percentage will not increase.

Q. Will my retirement pension from my job reduce the amount of my Social Security benefit?

A. If your pension is from work where you paid Social Security taxes, it will not affect the amount of your Social Security benefit. Pensions based on work that is not covered by Social Security (for example, the Federal civil service and some State or local government agencies) probably will cause the amount of your Social Security benefit to be reduced. This type of benefit reduction is called the "Windfall Elimination Provision (WEP). If you will receive a pension for work not covered by Social Security (such as government employment), any Social Security benefits you may be eligible to receive on your spouse's record may also be reduced. This type of benefit reduction is called "Government Pension Offset" (GPO).

Q. If I receive a government pension, how will this affect my Social Security benefits?

A. If you worked in a job that was not covered under Social Security, e.g., some Federal, State, or local government employment, the pension you get based on that work may reduce your Social Security benefits. Your benefit can be reduced under one of two provisions.

The first, called "government pension offset," applies only if you receive a government pension and are eligible for Social Security benefits as a spouse or widow(er). Under this provision, your Social Security benefit may be reduced by two-thirds of the amount of your government pension. There are several exceptions to this rule.

The other provision, called the "windfall elimination provision," affects how your Social Security retirement or disability benefits are figured if you also receive a pension from work not covered by Social Security. The formula used to figure your benefit amount is modified, giving you a lower Social Security benefit.

Social Security benefits are based on a worker's average monthly earnings adjusted for inflation. When they figure your benefits, they separate your average earnings into three amounts and multiply the figures using three factors. For example, for a worker who turns 62 in 2007, the first $680 of average monthly earnings is multiplied by 90 percent; the next $3,420 is multiplied by 32 percent; the remainder by 15 percent.

For more information, see Online WEP Calculator on website http://www.socialsecurity.gov/retire2/anyPiaWepjs04.htm.

Under the windfall elimination provision, your benefit under a modified formula in which the 90 percent factor is reduced to 40 percent is figured out. There are exceptions to this rule. For example, the 90 percent factor is not reduced if you have 30 or more years of "substantial" earnings in a job where you paid Social Security taxes. If you have 21 to 29 years of substantial earnings, the 90 percent factor is reduced to somewhere between 45 and 85 percent.

For more information, you should read the Social Security fact sheets "Government Pension Offset" (Publication No. 05-10007) and The Windfall Elimination Provision" (Publication No. 05-10045).

Computation of Benefits

Cost-of-Living Adjustment (COLA):

A Social Security cost-of-living (COLA) increase of 3.3% for 2007 was announced on October 18, 2006. It is effective January 1, 2007:

Based on the increase in the Consumer Price Index (CPI-W) from the third quarter of 2005 through the third quarter of 2006, Social Security and Supplemental Security Income (SSI) beneficiaries will receive a 3.3 percent COLA for 2007.

Other important 2007 Social Security information is provided in the following table.

Tax, Benefit and Earning Amounts for 2007

Notes	2006	2007
Tax Rate:		
Employee	7.65%	7.65%
Self-Employed	15.30%	15.30%
Note: The 7.65% tax rate is the combined rate for Social Security and Medicare. The Social Security portion (OASDI) is 6.20% on earnings up to the applicable taxable maximum amount. The Medicare portion (HI) is 1.45% on all earnings.		
Maximum Earnings Taxable:		
Social Security (OASDI Only)	$94,200	$97,500
Medicare (HI only)	No Limit	No Limit
Quarter of Coverage:		
Income for one quarter	$970	$1,000
Retirement Earnings Test Exempt Amounts:		
Before full retirement age	$12,480/yr	$12,960/yr
Note: One dollar in benefits will be withheld for every $2 in earnings above the limit	($1,040/mo)	($1,080/mo)
Retirement Earnings Test Exempt Amounts:		
The year you reach full retirement age	$33,240/yr	$34,440/yr
Note: Applies only to earnings for months prior to attaining full retirement age. One dollar in benefits will be withheld for every $3 in earnings above the limit.	($2770/mo)	($2,870/mo)
There is no limit on earnings beginning the month an individual attains full retirement age (65 and 8 months for retirees born in 1941; 65 and 10 months for those born in 1942).		

Computation of Benefits

Notes	2006	2007
Social Security Disability Thresholds:		
Substantial Gainful Activity (SGA) Non-Blind	$860/mo.	$900/mo.
Substantial Gainful Activity (SGA) Blind	$1,450/mo	$1,500/mo
Trial Work Period (TWP)	$620/mo.	$640/mo
Maximum Social Security Benefit:	$2,053/mo	$2,116/mo
Full Retirement Age	65 yr 8 mo	65 yr 10 mo
Note: For retirees born in 1941, full retirement age is 65 and 8 months; for those born in 1942 it is 65 and 10 months. Full retirement age will gradually increase to age 67 for those born in 1960 and later.		
SSI Federal Payment Standard:		
Individual	$603/mo	$623/mo
Couple	$904/mo	$934/mo
SSI Resources Limits:		
Individual	$2000/mo	$2000/mo
Couple	$3000/mo	$3000/mo

Estimated Average Monthly Social Security Benefits Payable in January 2007 Before and After 3.3% Cola

Category	Before	After
All Retired Workers	$1,011	$1,044
Aged Couple, Both Receiving Benefits	$1,658	$1,713
Widowed Mother and Two Children	$2,098	$2,167
Aged Widow(er) Alone	$976	$1,008
Disabled Worker, Spouse and One or More Children	$1,593	$1,646
All Disabled Workers	$947	$979

Check Payment Direct-Deposit Questions

Q. After I sign up for direct deposit, do I have to stay with the same bank?

A. No, you can use direct deposit at any bank, savings and loan or credit union. If you open a new account, you can sign up for Direct Deposit by, obtaining a password and "starting or changing direct deposit online (Social Security benefits only), or Contacting your bank, credit union or savings and loan association, or Calling Social Security toll-free at 1-800-772-1213 (TTY 1-800-325-0778), or filling out a "direct Deposit signup Form" and taking it to your financial institution or Social Security office.

When you contact the Social Security office, be sure to have your Social Security number and a personal check or statement from your new account. It is recommended that you wait until deposits are going to your new bank, savings and loan or credit union before you close your old account.

Q. Do I have to use direct deposit if my bank requires me to keep a minimum balance in order to open a checking account?

A. No, you can continue to get a check if using direct deposit is not right for you. But, you should continue to look for an account that suits your needs. The Department of the Treasury recently introduced an easy and

Check Payment Direct-Deposit Questions

affordable option to get Social Security benefits by direct deposit, called the Electronic Transfer Account (ETA).

The ETA is available through participating federally insured financial institutions, including banks, savings and loans and credit unions. For more information about the ETA or to locate an ETA provider, you should contact the ETA call center at 1-888-382-3311 or you can visit the Department of the Treasury's ETA website at http://www.eta-find.gov.

Q. What are the benefits of using direct deposit?

A. The benefits of using direct deposit are:

- It's safe.
- There are no checks to be lost or stolen.
- It's convenient.
- It's secure
- You will get your benefits on time, even if you're out of town, sick or unable to get to the bank.
- You are in control of your money.
- You choose the account where your Social Security payment is deposited.

Q. Can foreign beneficiaries use direct deposit?

A. You may wish your Social Security payment to be deposited directly into your account at either a financial institution in the country where you live or a U.S. financial institution. But, even if you use the direct deposit service, you must still keep them informed of any change in your current residence address.

With direct deposit, you receive your payment much faster than if you are paid by check (usually 1 to 3 weeks faster than check deliveries). When direct deposit payments are sent to a financial institution, you also avoid check cashing and currency conversion fees.

To determine if direct deposit is available in the country where you live or to sign up for direct deposit, contact the nearest U.S. Embassy or consulate or U.S. Social Security office, or write to the:

Social Security Administration
P.O. Box 17769
Baltimore, Maryland 21235-7769
USA

Earnings and Employment Questions

Q. What is the maximum wage contribution for Social Security in 2007, and what amount constitutes a credit (a quarter of coverage) for 2007?

A. The maximum wage contribution for 2007 was increased to $97,500 from $94,200 for 2006. The amount of earnings required to earn one credit has also increased to $1,000 per calendar quarter for 2007 from $970 per calendar quarter for 2006.

The 2007 contribution rate, also known as FICA tax, for employees and for self-employed people are, the 7.65% rate is the combined rate for Social Security and Medicare for employees. The Social Security portion (OASDI, or Old Age, Survivors and Disability Insurance) is 6.20% on earnings and the Medicare portion (HI) is 1.45% on all earnings. FICA tax contribution rate for Self employed person is double the employee rate (15.30%).

Q. How can I obtain a history of all my employers? I have applied for a job that requires me to provide a complete history of all employers for which I have worked. How can I obtain this report?

A. To obtain a detailed statement of your employment history, you need to complete Form SSA-7050-F4, Request For Social Security Earnings Information.

Under most circumstances there is a charge involved for detailed earnings information. Considerable clerical handling is required to prepare this information. Unlike the earnings information used to compute Social Security benefits, which is electronically available, detailed earnings information must be extracted from microfilmed records through a tedious, labor-intensive operation requiring visual examination of each record before a statement can be produced and released. SSA do not charge for providing more detailed earnings information for correcting a Social Security record or for establishing entitlement to Social Security benefits.

The Social Security Administration does not charge a fee for providing individuals with a statement showing yearly totals of earnings, the amount of Social Security taxes paid, an estimate of future benefits, and the number of credits you have under the Social Security program. Normally, this is all the information that is needed to determine Social Security benefits. You may obtain a Social Security Statement at http://www.socialsecurity.gov/statement.

Earnings and Employment Questions

Q. How can I check my Social Security earnings for accuracy?

A. It is important that you review page 3 of the Social Security Statement you receive each year to make sure the earnings record is correct and that social security department have recorded each year that you worked. You are the only person who can look at the earnings chart and know whether it is complete and correct. If your records are wrong, you may not receive all the benefits to which you are entitled.

If some, or all, of your earnings from the last year are not shown on your Statement, it could be that they were processing last year's earnings reports when your Statement was prepared. Your complete earnings for the last year will be shown on the next Statement you receive. Call on 1-800-772-1213 (7 a.m. - 7 p.m. your local time) if any earnings for years before last year are shown incorrectly. If possible, have your W-2 or tax return for those years available.

Self Employment Questions

Q. I am self-employed. How do I pay Social Security tax?

A. The majority of people who pay into Social Security work for someone else. Their employer deducts Social Security taxes from their paycheck, matches that contribution and sends wage reports and taxes to the Internal Revenue Service (IRS) and Social Security. But self-employed people must report their earnings and pay the taxes directly to the IRS.

You are self-employed if you operate a trade, business or profession, either by yourself or as a partner. You report your earnings for Social Security when you file your federal income tax return. If your net earnings are $400 or more in a taxable year, you must report your earnings on Schedule SE for Social Security coverage purposes, in addition to the other tax forms you must file, the Social Security tax rate for 2007 is 15.3 percent (the same as 2006) on self-employment income up to $97,500. If your net earnings exceed $97,500, you continue to pay only the Medicare portion of the Social Security tax, which is 2.9 percent, on the rest of your earnings. There are two income tax deductions that reduce your tax liability. The deductions are intended to make sure self-employed people are treated in much the same way as employers and employees for Social Security and income tax purposes.

First, your net earnings from self-employment are reduced by an amount equal to half of your total Social Security tax. This is similar to the way employees are treated under the tax laws in that the employer's share of the Social Security tax is not considered income to the employee.

Self Employment Questions

Second, you can deduct half of your Social Security tax on the IRS Form 1040 (line 29). This means the deduction is taken from your gross income in determining adjusted gross income. It cannot be an itemized deduction and must not be listed on your Schedule C.

If you have wages as well as self-employment earnings, the tax on your wages is paid first. But this rule is important only if your total earnings are more than $97,500. For example, if you have $20,000 in wages and $30,000 in self-employment income in 2007, you pay the appropriate Social Security taxes on both your wages and business earnings. However, if your 2006 wages are $100,000 and you have $10,000 in net earnings from a business, you do not pay dual Social Security taxes on earnings above $97,500. Your employer will withhold 7.65 percent in Social Security taxes up to $97,500 and 1.45 percent (the Medicare portion of an employee's tax rate) on earnings between $97,500 and $100,000. And you must pay the 2.9 percent Medicare self-employment tax (not the full Social Security tax) on your $10,000 in self-employment earnings.

Q. What is the Social Security contribution rate for 2007?

A. The 2006 contribution rate; also known as the FICA tax rate, is 7.65% for employees, and 15.30% for self-employed People. The rates are broken out as follows:

- 6.2% (Social Security portion) on earnings up to the maximum taxable amount ($97,500 in 2007).

- 1.45% (Medicare portion) on all earnings (total yearly income).

Q. Can I buy additional Social Security credits? I only have 36 credits and need four more credits to qualify for

Self Employment Questions

Social Security benefits. Can I contribute money to Social Security to earn the additional credits?

A. No. People cannot get additional Social Security credits by voluntarily contributing money to Social Security. They can earn credits only by working in a job or business or as a self-employed person, covered under Social Security by paying social security taxes.

Q. Will I pay more in social security taxes if I am self employed? I may open a small business. Will I pay more in Social Security taxes than I did when I worked for someone else?

A. A self-employed person pays twice as much as an employee pays. However, because the employer pays a matching amount, the combined rate paid by the employer and the employee is equal to the self-employment tax. But there are special tax credits you can take when you file your tax return that are intended to lower your overall rate.

In 2006, the Social Security tax rate is 15.3 percent on self-employment income up to $94,200. For 2007 the tax rate is 15.3 percent on income up to $97,500. Although you do not pay self-employment tax on net earnings exceeding $94,200 (or $97,500), you must continue to pay the Medicare portion of the Social Security tax (2.9 percent) on the rest of your earnings.

Self Employment Questions

Q. I no longer work in the U.S.A. Can I have a Social Security tax refund? I have worked in the USA for less than 40 quarters and paid Social Security taxes while living in the U.S. Since I am not eligible to receive Social Security benefits, can I have a refund of the taxes I paid?

A. The law does not permit a refund of Social Security taxes.

However, you may be eligible to receive U.S. Social Security benefits as a result of a bilateral agreement between the U.S. and your resident country. These agreements help many people who, without the agreement, would not be eligible for monthly retirement, disability or survivor's benefits under the Social Security systems of one or both countries. These agreements also help people who would otherwise have to pay taxes to both countries on the same earnings. You may access information about the agreements between the United States and other

Q. How do I request copies of W-2's from previous years?

A. IRS will provide copies of W-2 for a previous year if a tax return was filed and if the request is for Federal tax purposes or related to Federal tax situations. IRS maintains W-2 information for the current tax year and previous 9 years. SSA cannot provide W-2 copies for any earlier years. If a copy of the W-2 is needed for federal tax purposes, contact your local IRS Service center or contact IRS at its national toll-free number 1-800-829-1040.

SSA will provide copies of W-2 at no charge, if the W-2 is needed for SSA program purposes, i.e., there is a question of the earnings posted to the individual's social security earnings record. SSA will provide copies of W-2 for non-SSA program related purposes, however SSA will charge a fee for providing the W-2.

Self Employment Questions

Some examples of non-SSA-program purpose are:

* Filing federal or state tax returns.
* Resolving state tax discrepancies.
* Establishing residency.
* Lost form; and
* Pension funds.

A fee of $30 will be charged for each year that copies of Forms W-2 are requested, regardless of the number of W-2 copies actually provided for each of the years requested, or whether copies are available for the year(s) requested.

Copies of W-2s from SSA can be made using either IRS Form 4506 (Request for copy or Transcript of Tax Form) or other written correspondence. The request should be sent to:

Social Security Administration
Office of Central Operations Division of Earnings Records Operations
P.O. Box 33003
Baltimore, MD 21290-3003

When you write to SSA, be sure to include the following information:

* Social Security number,
* Name shown on your Social Security card
* Any different names shown on your W-2
* Complete mailing address
* Year(s) that you are requesting copies of the Form W-2.

Self Employment Questions

- Daytime telephone number
- Reason for the request.

Q. Is there a time limit for correcting my earnings record?

A. The Social Security Act defines the basic statute of limitations beyond which earnings ordinarily may not be corrected is 3 years, 3 months, and 15 days after the close of the taxable year in which wages are paid or SEI is derived. However, the Act also defines exceptions to protect Social Security contributors from unfair treatment because of any delay on the part of the Social Security Administration in processing earnings. The exceptions permit SSA to correct errors after the statute has expired and include authority for them to:

- Confirm records with tax returns filed with the Internal Revenue Service.
- Correct errors due to employee omissions from processed employer reports or missing reports.
- Correct errors "on the face of the record," that is, errors SSA can find by examining their records of processed reports; and
- Include wages reported by an employer as paid to an individual but not shown in their records.

Q. If I am self-employed, will my earnings limit be before or after expenses?

A. Social Security only considers your net earnings from self-employment, as reported on Schedule C and Schedule SE of your tax return.

Forms and Publications Questions

Q. How do I get copies of Social Security's publications?

A. A complete directory to all of the information pamphlets and fact sheets that SSA publishes on its benefits programs including Retirement, Disability, Medicare, Supplemental Security Income, Survivors benefits, and information about your Social Security Number are available at Social Security Benefit Publications on website http://www.socialsecurity.gov/pubs/englist.html.

You may download and print the publications from your personal computer. Social Security now has another way to send public information. You can request information documents from Social Security through SSA's Fax Catalog. Documents include fact sheets about various aspects of Social Security programs, information in Spanish, research tables and actuarial reports. If you have a touch-tone phone and access to a FAX machine, you can use FAX Catalog. Call toll-free, 1-888-475-7000, to get an index or request copies of publications in several languages. When you call, a voice menu leads you through the steps to receive your information. When you call, you must know the FAX number where you will receive the information.

If you want large quantities of SSA publications, you can send a written request to:

Social Security Administration
Office of Supply and Warehouse Management

Forms and Publications Questions

239 Supply Building
6301 Security Blvd Baltimore, MD 21235

The phone number for the Public Information Distribution Center is (410) 965-2039. You can also reach them via fax at (410) 965-2037. You may also call toll-free number, 1-800-772-1213 and request any pamphlets you desire. People who are deaf or hard of hearing may call toll-free TTY number, 1-800-325-0778, between 7 a.m. and 7 p.m. on Monday through Friday or email them at oplm.oswm.rpt.orders@ssa.gov.

Q. What benefit publications are available online?

A. Social Security (SSA) has more than 150 publications in English, Spanish and other languages that you can read and print.

Read a list of "SSA Publications in English on website

http://www.socialsecurity.gov/pubs

Read a list of Publications in Spanish; on web site
http://www.socialsecurity.gov/espanol/publist2.html

If you are looking for a Medicare publication, go to the Medicare website http://www.medicare.gov/Publications

International Questions

Q. I live outside of the U.S. How do I contact Social Security?

A. If you are in Canada, British Virgin Islands or Samoa, you may obtain services from an SSA Field Office.

In countries where there are a relatively large number of Social Security customers, American embassies and consulates have personnel who have been specially trained to provide a full range of services, including the taking of applications for benefits.

For phone numbers and addresses of offices serving customers outside of the U.S. see Service Around the world on website http://www.socialsecurity.gov/foreign

You may also write at following address:

Social Security Administration
Office of International Operations
P.O. Box 17775
Baltimore, Maryland 21235-7775

Q. Can noncitizens receive Social Security benefits?

A. In many cases, yes

International Questions

To qualify for benefits, all noncitizens first must meet the same eligibility requirements as U.S. citizens. Additionally, a noncitizen worker assigned a Social Security number (SSN) on or after January 1, 2004, must meet another eligibility requirement. If you are subject to this provision, neither you nor your dependents can qualify for benefits based on your earnings unless at some point, you were assigned an SSN based on your authorization to work in the United States, or at some point, you were admitted to this country as a nonimmigrant business visitor (B-1) or as an alien crewman (D-1 or D-2).

Once a noncitizen worker has met eligibility criteria, he/she must have evidence of the "lawful presence" of the beneficiary. That means that before they can pay out benefits for any given month, Social Security must have evidence that during that month the beneficiary was either:

- A U.S. citizen;
- A U.S. national; or
- Lawfully present in the United States.

Several electronic publications offer more details about eligibility. Requirements and other issues affecting noncitizens are available on website http://socialsecurity.gov/pubs/englist.html

Q. I am a US citizen but plan to live overseas. Can I collect Social Security benefits in a foreign country?

A. If you are a U.S. citizen, you may receive your Social Security payments outside the U.S. as long as you are eligible for them. Regardless of your citizenship, there are certain countries where they are not allowed to send payments. For more information, please visit website at http://www.socialsecurity.gov/pubs/10137.html.

International Questions

Q. How do I get an Individual Taxpayer Identification Number?

A. The Internal Revenue Service (IRS) assigns Individual Taxpayer Identification Numbers (ITINs), not the Social Security Administration. The IRS assigns ITINs to certain nonresident and resident aliens, their spouses and dependents. You can use an ITIN for Federal tax purposes only. You cannot use it to work. Only non-citizens who are ineligible for a Social Security number can get an ITIN.

If you apply for a Social Security number and social security department cannot currently assign one to you, they will send you a letter of explanation in the mail. If they cannot assign you a Social Security number and you need an ITIN, you will need to file Form W-7 with the IRS.

Q. If I leave the US, can I continue to receive benefits?

A. If you are a United States citizen, you can travel or live in most foreign countries without affecting your eligibility for Social Security benefits.

However, there are a few countries like Cambodia, Cuba, North Korea, Vietnam and many of the former U.S.S.R. republics (except Armenia, Estonia, Latvia, Lithuania and Russia), where they cannot send Social Security checks.

If you are not a United States citizen, the law requires them to stop your payments after you have been outside the United States for six calendar months unless you meet one of several exceptions in the law, which will permit you to continue receiving benefits abroad. These exceptions are based, for the most part, on your citizenship.

International Questions

For example, if you are entitled to worker's benefits and are a citizen of one of the many countries with which the United States has a reciprocal arrangement to pay each other's citizens in another country, your Social Security benefits may continue after you leave the United States.

If you work outside the United States, different rules apply in determining if you can get your benefit checks. Most people who are neither U.S. residents nor U.S. citizens will have 25.5 percent of their benefits withheld for federal income tax.

For more information about receiving benefits abroad, read the booklet, "Payments While You Are Outside the United States" (Publication No.05-10137) from website at http://www.socialsecurity.gov/pubs/10137.html.

Q. Will Medicare cover my medical expenses outside of the U.S.?

A. Persons living or traveling outside the United States usually cannot benefit from Medicare. This is because, generally speaking, the program provides protection against the cost of hospital and medical expenses incurred in the United States.

There are rare emergency cases where Medicare can pay for care in Canada or Mexico. Also, Medicare can sometimes pay if a Canadian or Mexican hospital is closer to your home than the nearest U.S. hospital that can provide the care you need. If you get emergency treatment in a Canadian or Mexican hospital or if you live near one, ask someone who works at the hospital about Medicare coverage, or have the hospital help you contact the Medicare Intermediary.

Health insurance protection may be very important to anyone temporarily abroad who plans to return to the United States. If you plan to return to the United States shortly after you are eligible for the medical insurance program, you may wish to enroll during your first enrollment period. If you expect to be abroad for a longer period of time, you may wish to enroll during a later general enrollment period.

A general enrollment period is held January 1 through March 31 of each year. Your protection will begin July 1 of the year you enroll. If you enroll during a general enrollment period, your monthly premium may be increased by 10 percent for each 12-month period you could have had medical insurance coverage but were not enrolled. You will have to pay this extra amount as long as you have Part B.

Note: If you are covered by an employer or union group health plan through you or your spouse's current or active employment, you may qualify for a special enrollment period.

Q. I have worked overseas. Can I apply this work to my Social Security record?

A. Your work overseas may help you to qualify for U.S. benefits if it was covered under a foreign Social Security system. The United States has Social Security agreements with a number of other countries. One of the main purposes of these agreements is to help people who have worked in both the United States and the other country, but who have not worked long enough in one country or the other to qualify for Social Security benefits.

Under the agreement, they can count your work credits in the other country if this will help you qualify for U.S. benefits. However, if you already have enough credits under U.S. Social Security to qualify for a benefit, social security will not count your credits in the other country. If they count your foreign work credits, you will receive a partial U.S. benefit that is related to the length of time you worked under U.S. Social Security.

International Questions

Although they may count your work credits in the other country, your credits are not actually transferred from that country to the United States. They remain on your record in the other country. It is therefore possible for you to qualify for a separate benefit payment from both countries.

For more information about the agreements, including details about specific agreements in force, see "International Agreements, Payments Outside United States, and Social Security in Other Countries" on website http://www.socialsecurity.gov/international

Q. I live outside the United States. Where do I file for retirement benefits?

A. Personnel in American embassies or consulates in several countries (and in the SSA Division of the Veterans Affairs Regional Office in Manila, Philippines) are specially trained to take applications for Social Security benefits. The U.S. Social Security offices near the Canadian border take claims filed by people living in Canada.

For more information on these offices and filing for benefits while you are abroad, on website http://www.socialsecurity.gov/foreign "Service around the world".

Laws and Regulations Questions

Q. How can I locate Social Security's Rules and Regulations?

A. Every April 1st, final rules, which take effect over the past year, are incorporated into the compilation of the "Code of Federal Regulations for Social security. For example, final rules, which took effect April 1, 2005, through March 31, 2006, were incorporated into the April 1, 2006, compilation. Also, this version incorporated final rules published prior to April 1, 2006, which had effective dates beyond April 1.

If you want to look at regulations that are in effect currently, you must look at both the "Code of Federal Regulations for Social Security, revised as of April 1, 2006, and the Final Rules April 1, 2006, to date, which have been published in the Federal Register. This will give you a complete regulatory picture.

Q. What does Title II under the Social Security Act pertain to and how is eligibility met?

A. Title II of the Social Security Act pertains to Federal Old-Age, Survivors, and Disability Insurance benefits. The Social Security program pays benefits to retired or disabled workers and their families, and to the families of deceased workers.

To be eligible for Social Security retirement benefits, an individual must be at least 62 years old, have worked, paid Social Security taxes, earned at least 40 credits (10 years of work) and apply.

Laws and Regulations Questions

To be eligible for Social Security disability benefits, an individual must be disabled (unable to engage in substantial gainful activity), earned a minimum number of credits from work covered under Social Security and apply. Generally, you need 20 credits earned in the last 10 years, ending with the year you became disabled. However, younger workers may qualify with fewer credits.

When a person dies, certain members of the family may be eligible for survivors' benefits if the deceased worked, paid Social Security taxes, and earned enough credits. The number of credits a person needs depends on their age at the time of death. The younger a person is, the fewer credits are needed for family members to be eligible for survivors' benefits. However, nobody needs more than 40 credits to be eligible for any Social Security benefit.

A former spouse can receive benefits under the same circumstances as a window/widower if the marriage lasted 10 years or more. Survivors benefits paid to a surviving divorced spouse will not affect the benefit rates for other survivors receiving benefits.

For more information, read, "Social security Retirement Benefits," publication number 05-10035, " Social Security Survivors Benefits" publication number 05-10084, and "Social Security Disability Benefits" publication number 05-10029.

You can access these and other publications on the Internet at web site at http:// www.socialsecurity.gov/pubs.

Q. What Federal law gives the Commissioner of Social Security the authority to issue regulations?

A. Three sections of the Social Security Act give the Commissioner of Social Security broad statutory authority to issue regulations. They are sections 205(a) (title II), 1631(d)(1) (title XVI), and 702(a)(5) (title VII).

Laws and Regulations Questions

In addition, several other sections (e.g., section 1631(a)) give the Commissioner specific authority to issue regulations on particular topics. The regulations the Commissioner issues are subject to the rulemaking procedures established under section 553 of title 5, United States Code.

Q. How can I find out about job opportunities at the Social Security Administration?

A. Information about SSA current employment opportunities can be found on the "Social Security Careers" Home page at http://www.socialsecurity.gov/careers.

The Office of Personnel Management also provides information about jobs at Federal Government agencies, including the Social Security Administration (SSA), on the Internet at http://www.usajobs.opm.gov.

Part 2
Information from POMS

The Program Operations Manual System (POMS)

The Program Operations Manual System (POMS) is a set of employee instructions on taking claims and paying benefits. Many parts use technical language, which may not be familiar to the general public. However, the detailed operational steps may be useful in understanding how Social Security Department apply the law and regulations in specific circumstances.

To access the POMS online, go to:

https://secure.ssa.gov/apps10/poms.nsf

Eligibility for Hospital Insurance (HI) HI 00801.131:

Requirements for Entitlement:

To become entitled to Premium-HI, an individual must have attained age 65 (see GN 00302.005);

And be a resident of the U.S. and either:

* A citizen or an alien lawfully admitted for permanent residence who has resided in the U.S. continuously for the 5-year period immediately preceding the month all other requirements are met; (see GN 00303.000ff); And

* Be ineligible for HI under any other provision; and already have SMI (Supplementary Medical Insurance) coverage ;OR

* Be eligible for SMI enrollment and file an enrollment request which will entitle him to SMI (see HI 00801.136C. and D.) and

* File an application for HI during a prescribed enrollment period (see HI 00801.136).

Mandatory SMI (Supplementary Medical Insurance) Coverage:

An individual may not enroll in Premium-HI without an existing or simultaneous enrollment in SMI. Further, the termination of an

Eligibility for Hospital Insurance (HI) HI 00801.131:

individual's SMI coverage requires a simultaneous termination of Premium-HI coverage.

First Month of eligibility QMB/SLMB/QI:

The first month of eligibility is usually the month the individual attains age 65. However, the first month of eligibility is later than age 65 in the following situations.

The person first meets the citizenship/residency requirements after he attains age 65.

An individual's initial enrollment period (IEP) begins 3 months before such first month and continues for 7 months.

Enrollment and coverage periods (HI 00801.133):

Basic Rules for Enrollment:

An individual who is not subject to Part A buy-in as discussed in (see HI 00801.140)may only enroll for Premium-HI during the following periods:

Initial Enrollment Period (IEP):

The IEP begins 3 months before the first month of eligibility (generally, the month of attainment of age 65; (see HI 00801.131. C for exceptions) and continues for 7 months. Coverage based on an IEP enrollment begins as provided for in (see HI 00805.165). The IEP for Premium-HI is generally the same as the IEP for SMI.

General Enrollment Period (GEP):

The GEP is January through March of each year. Coverage based on a GEP enrollment begins the following July 1.

Special Enrollment Period (SEP):

The SEP is an enrollment opportunity for individuals whose employer group health plan coverage based on current employment has ended. (see HI 00805.266ff for a complete discussion of the SEP provisions.)

Enrollment and coverage periods (HI 00801.133):

Transfer Enrollment Period:

This is a special enrollment opportunity for Medicare beneficiaries who are also Health Maintenance Organization (HMO) or Competitive Medical Plan (CMP) enrollees and whose HMO or CMP enrollment is terminated either on a voluntary basis or because of termination of the HMO or CMP contract. (see HI 00801.143 for further discussion.)

Joint Bank Account

Cases have reported to SSA of their harassment by welfare staff for their joint accounts with their children or other relatives.

The P.O.M.S has following advice to give:

The most common causes of "joint account "problems can be avoided by advising clients as early as possible what assets count as resources to them. In joint account situation it is important to obtain written statements from the co-owner(s) of the account showing that the claimant did not own and did not use all or a portion of the funds. It is also essential to have written proof that the account has been changed to reflect the claimant's non-access or limited access thereto. Whether a claimant is able to rebut the presumption of joint ownership usually turns on his/her credibility.

A bank account bearing an SSI recipient's Social security number, will inevitably have an adverse impact on his or her eligibility when the existence of the account becomes known to social security even though the SSI recipient may not consider the funds belong to him or her e.g.. The account contains someone else's money, which would only become available to the SSI recipient if something happened to the other person.

It may also be noted that if a welfare claimant has in his account somebody else's money, the presumption would be that it is his own money. It is not possible to rebut their presumption

The instructions in SI 01140.200, except for those in SI 01140.200A.1 (ownership), apply to all checking and savings accounts. The instructions

Joint Bank Account

in this section, which apply to joint accounts only, supplement those in SI 0140.200.

Reference: SI 01140.205 Joint Checking and Savings Accounts.

Procedure –Rebuttable Ownership Assumption

Account Holders Include One or More Claimants or Recipients and No Deemors

Assume that all the funds in the account belong to the claimant(s)/recipient(s), in equal shares if there is more than one claimant or recipient.

Account Holders Include One or More Deemors.

Provided that none of the account holders is a claimant or recipient (in which case the assumption in SI 01140.205b.1 would apply), assume that all the funds in the account belong to the deemor(s), in equal shares if there is more than one deemor.

Temporary Absence From the State

A temporary absence occurs when a recipient leaves the State without the intention of abandoning his or her residency.

Absent evidence to the contrary, SSA assume that an absence from the State lasting 90 or fewer calendar days is a temporary absence.

Exception: The 90-day limit for temporary absences does not apply to an absence from the State to reside in an institution. Absent evidence to the contrary, SSA assumes that an absence to reside in an institution is temporary, regardless of its duration. (see SI 00520.010 defines institution & SI 00520.100 defines resident of an institution.)

Establishing Absence and Presence in the U.S. (RS 02610.020):

1. Full Consecutive Calendar Months:

To determine a 6 full consecutive calendar month period (see 3. below), look no further back than to the last day of the 7th month before the first month of entitlement. Once an alien is considered as being outside the U.S. for 30 consecutive days, the 6-month period of absence is measured from the first day of the first full month of absence. Only a return to the U.S. of at least 30 consecutive days will cause a break in the 6-month period of absence. If the 6-month period is broken, it will not start again until the alien again leaves the U.S. for at least 30 consecutive days.

Example: Hugh Fitzhugh, an alien, has resided outside the U.S. continuously since 1984. He visits the U.S for one day on September 8, 1988 and files a claim for monthly benefits. His first month of entitlement is October 1988, the month he attains age 65. Alien suspension will be effective October 1988 unless he spends the full calendar month of October 1988 in the U.S. In determining his status, SSA look no further back than to the last day of the 7th month before the first month of entitlement. He was not in the U.S. at any time from April 1, 1988 through April 30, 1988 and subsequently has not been in the U.S. for 30 consecutive days. Therefore, he is not now considered to be in the U.S.

Establishing Absence and Presence in the U.S. (RS 02610.020):

2. Resumption Of Payment:

Once the 6-month period of absence is completed and payments suspended, payments may not be resumed until the alien has been back in the U.S. for one full calendar month. Payments will be resumed effective with the first full calendar month throughout which the beneficiary is in the U.S.

3. Full Calendar Month/30 Consecutive Days:

Do not confuse the requirement to spend a full calendar month in the U.S for resumption of payments after being suspended with the requirement that a beneficiary spend 30 full consecutive days in the U.S. to interrupt a 6-month period of absence. The two requirements are not interchangeable; e.g., payments may be resumed (after suspension for 6 months absence) if the beneficiary spends the entire month of February in the U.S. Presence in the U.S. for the full month of February (28 days) does not interrupt a 6-month period of absence.

A "full calendar month" means all of the first day of the calendar month through all of the last day of such month. A presence of "30 consecutive days" means presence for 24 hours of each and every day of a consecutive 30-day period.

Payment to Aliens living outside USA

Exemptions from Section 202(t)(11) of the Social Security Act (the Act).

Under section 202(t)(11) of the Act, dependents or survivors benefits generally may not be paid to aliens outside the United States who first become eligible for the benefits after 1984, unless they satisfy certain U.S. residency requirements. However, citizens or residents of an agreement country are exempt from these requirements unless an agreement includes a limitation on the exemption. The individual agreement subchapters explain whether any limitation applies.

When the beneficiary is not a citizen of an agreement country but resides in an agreement country, the exemption is effective beginning with the month after the month the beneficiary becomes a resident of the agreement country, but no earlier than the effective date of the agreement, and terminates the month after the month in which the beneficiary abandons residence in the agreement country (continued payment is then based on the regular alien nonpayment provisions).

References:

Section 202(t)(1) alien nonpayment provisions, RS 02610.001

Section 202(t)(11) alien nonpayment provisions, RS 02610.025

Example: Outside U.S. For 30 Days But Not For Any Calendar Month

Mr. Benes left the U.S. on July 1 and returned on August 1. Counting July 2 through July 31, he was outside the U.S. for 30 consecutive days and his period of absence from the U.S. continues for another 30 consecutive days. Beginning with the day of return and counting through August 30, he was not absent for any full calendar month. Thus, he is eligible for payments for July and August.

Example: Outside U.S. For Calendar Month But Less Than 30 Days (February Only)

Ms. Johnson left the U.S. on January 31 and returned on March 1. Counting February 1 through February 28, she was absent for the full calendar month of February and thus was ineligible for that month. Because the absence was for less than 30 consecutive days, the period of absence ends the day before her actual return; therefore, she was again eligible for payment beginning with March 1

ALIENS Non-Payment Exemptions (GN 01701.150)

Exemptions from Alien Nonpayment Provisions of the Social Security Act (the Act)

Section 202(t)(1) of the Act generally provides that benefits for certain alien beneficiaries will be suspended once they are outside the United States for 6 months. The Act exempts certain beneficiaries from suspension for periods when they reside in an agreement country. The individual agreement subchapters explain what categories of alien beneficiaries are exempt under each agreement. The exemption, applies to such beneficiaries entitled to U.S. Totalization or non-Totalization benefits, is effective beginning with the month after the month such beneficiary becomes a resident of an agreement country (but not earlier than the effective date of the agreement), terminates the month after the month such beneficiary abandons residence in an agreement country (continued payment is then based on the regular alien nonpayment provisions), and applies to the lump-sum death payment provided, the number holder (NH) resided in an agreement country at the time of death, the NH's death occurred in the month following the month the agreement in the NH's country of residence became effective or later, and the deceased NH was eligible for monthly benefits for the month prior to the month of death.

Gifts (SI 00830.520)

1. Definition of Gift:

A gift is something a person receives which is not repayment for goods or services the person provided and is not given because of a legal obligation on the giver's part.

To be a gift, something must be given irrevocably (i.e., the donor relinquishes all control).

"Donations" and "contributions" may meet the definition of a gift.

A gift received as the result of a death is a death benefit. (See SI 00830.545.)

2. Gift as Income:

A gift is unearned income subject to the general rules pertaining to income and income exclusions.

Reminder: The value of any noncash item (other than food, or shelter) is not income if the item would become a partially or totally excluded nonliquid resource if retained in the month after the month of receipt. (See SI 00815.550).

Gifts (SI 00830.520)

3. Gifts Used to Pay Tuition, Fees, or Other Necessary Educational Expenses:

For benefits Payable on or after June 1, 2004 Gifts (or a portion of a gift) used to pay for tuition, fees, or other necessary educational expenses at any educational institution, including vocational and technical education, are excluded from income. (See SI 00830.455).

Gifts (or a portion of a gift) used to pay for tuition, fees, or other necessary educational expenses at any educational institution, including vocational and technical education, are excluded from resources for the 9-month period beginning the month after the month the gift was received. (See SI 01130.455).

Gifts of Travel Tickets (SI 00830.521):

Definition of Domestic and Non-Domestic Travel

Domestic Travel:

Domestic travel is travel in or between the 50 States, the District of Columbia, Puerto Rico, the U.S. Virgin Islands, Guam, American Samoa, and the Northern Mariana Islands.

Non-Domestic Travel:

Non-domestic travel is travel to any place other than those listed in SI 00830.521A.1

POLICY for Gift:

1. Gift of Domestic Travel Ticket Not Converted To Cash.

The value of a ticket for domestic travel received by an individual, or his/her spouse, or parent whose income is subject to deeming is excluded from income if:

the ticket is received as a gift (SI 00830.521); and the ticket is not converted to cash (e.g., cashed in, sold, etc.). This policy applies to tickets for domestic travel received on or after 3/1/90.

Gifts of Travel Tickets (SI 00830.521):

2. Gift of Domestic Travel Ticket Converted to Cash

A domestic ticket received as a gift is treated as unearned income in the month the ticket was converted to cash.

3. Gift of Non-Domestic Travel Ticket.

The gift of a non-domestic travel ticket that cannot be converted to cash (i.e., it is not refundable) or used to obtain food, clothing, or shelter is not considered as income (SI 00815.001) even if the ticket was used for transportation. Travel tickets that can be converted are income and are counted as unearned income at the current market value (CMV) in the month of receipt (SI 00835.020 and SI 00835.310 C) whether or not the ticket was used for transportation.

Over Payments Waiver (GN 02250.001)

Recovery of an overpayment can be waived if both of the following conditions are met:

The person is without fault, and recovery would either defeat the purpose of the act or be against equity and good conscience.

Waiver Defeat the Purpose (GN 02250.100)

Recovery of an overpayment will defeat the purpose of title II of the Social Security Act if recovery would deprive the person of income required for ordinary and necessary living expenses.

Recovery will defeat the purpose of title II to the extent that the person does not have any of the overpaid funds in his possession when notified of the overpayment (GN 02250.105) and the person Receives cash public assistance (GN 02250.110); or

Needs substantially all current income to meet ordinary and necessary living expenses (GN 02250.120) and recovery would reduce assets below the levels specified in GN 02250.115A.4.

111

Treatment of Assets Under Income and Resources Rules.

When an individual receives something in cash or in kind during a month, SSA evaluates it under the appropriate income counting rules in that month. If the individual retains the item into the month following that of receipt, SSA evaluate it under the resource counting rules. Thus, SSA do not evaluate the same asset under two sets of counting rules for the same month.

Receipts form the Sale, Exchange , or Replacement of Resource.

If an individual sells, exchanges, or replaces a resource, what he/she receives in return is not income. It is a different form of resource. This includes assets, which have never been subject to resources counting because the owner sold, exchanged, or replaced them in the same month in which he/ she received them.

SI 00830.510 contains instructions on the income/resources treatment of proceeds received for timber, gravel, and other natural resources.

Example: Receipt of a Resource Considered as Income and Exchanged in the same month Miss Laramie, a disabled individual, received a $350 unemployment insurance benefit on January 10 at which time it was unearned income. On January 18, she used the $350 to purchase several shares of stock; i.e., she exchanged one resource (cash) for another resource (stock). SSA never counted the $350 cash payment as a resource because Miss Laramie exchanged it for stock in the month of receipt. The stock is not income; it is a different form of resource. Since a resource is not countable until the first moment of the month following its receipt, SSA first count the stock in the resources determination made as of February 1.

Assets that are not resources- Policy Principle and General Rules(SI 01110.115):

Assets of any kind are not resources if the individual does not have any ownership interest; and the legal right, authority, or power to liquidate them (provided they are not already in cash); or the legal right to use the assets for his/her support and maintenance.

Example: An individual owns a block of stock jointly with his brother. Although the form of ownership is one, which would permit either to sell the property without the other's consent, the brothers have a legally binding agreement that one will not sell without consent of the other. The individual's brother refuses his consent, thereby making the stock not a resource for the individual. However, if the brother should give his consent, the stock would be subject to evaluation under the resources-counting rules beginning with the month following the month of consent. The value of the stock would not be counted as income to the individual.

Qualifying Quarters (QQs)

QQs Earned by a Parent's Holding-Out Spouse:

QQs earned by the LAPR alien's natural/adoptive parent's holding-out spouse (defined in SI 00501.152 and developed per SI 00502.145B.3) during the time the holding-out relationship existed can be credited to the LAPR alien if at the time the determination of eligibility is made, the holding-out relationship continues to exist (i.e., the holding-out spouse lives with the natural/adoptive parent) and the LAPR alien is under age 18.

Example: An LAPR alien born 10/10/85 currently lives with his natural mother and an individual determined to be his natural mother's holding-out spouse. The holding-out spouse began living with the LAPR alien and his natural mother in 1/86. The QQs earned by the natural mother's holding-out spouse can be credited from 1/86 through the present since the holding-out relationship still exists and the LAPR alien is under age 18.

QQs Earned by a Current Spouse and/or One or More Deceased Spouses:

QQs earned by a current spouse and/or one or more deceased spouses during marriage to the LAPR alien can be credited. Develop the duration of marriage as necessary to accurately determine the number of QQs creditable. (See SI 00502.145).

Example: An LAPR alien's current spouse has earned 20 QQs since married to the LAPR alien, and the LAPR alien's former spouse who died while married to the LAPR alien earned over 20 QQs during the marriage. The LAPR alien can be credited with the QQs from both spouses and therefore qualify based on this provision.

Note: Eligibility based on the credit of QQs from a deceased spouse is not lost if the LAPR alien remarries.

Current-Year QQs:

Current year earnings can be used to help establish 40 QQs to determine eligibility under this provision. However, current year QQs can be assigned only to past and current calendar quarters, one per calendar quarter per worker. A QQ is acquired on the first day of the quarter in which it is assigned per RS 00301.230.

If an otherwise eligible individual's earnings permit the 40th QQ to be credited during the life of the application (see SI 00601.010), eligibility can be found based on current year earnings no earlier than the first month of the calendar quarter to which the 40th QQ is assigned. For claims filed 8/22 /96 or later, benefits are payable beginning the first day of the month following the later of the date the individual files the application or becomes eligible (SI 00601.009)

Example: An aged LAPR alien files an SSI application on 03/2/97. He does not meet the 40 QQ determinations in 03/97 as he can only be credited with 39 QQs, 20 QQs of his own and 19 earned by his current wife during their marriage. He meets all other eligibility factors in March and subsequent months. The SSA made the input to the system on 03/15/97 to deny his claim. The life of his application would have ended on March 15; however, he filed a timely request for reconsideration on 04/30/97.

Qualifying Quarters (QQs)

In 04/97, his wife earned $700, enough for 1 QQ. The QQ can be credited as of 04/1/97, giving her a total of 20 QQs. On 05/15/97, the Field officer (FO) made the reconsideration decision and determined that the LAPR alien did not meet the 40 QQ determination for March but that he did meet it beginning 04/01/97 since as of April 1, he can be credited with 20 QQs of his own and 20 from his wife. The FO made the input to the system on 05/15/97 to pay the LAPR alien SSI benefits beginning 05/1/97 (the first day of the month following the date he became eligible), based on the 03/2/97 application.

"Similar Fault" Definition

"Similar fault" exists when an SSI recipient or other person knowingly makes an incorrect or incomplete statement that is material to the determination for SSI payments or knowingly conceals information that is material to the determination of eligibility or amount of SSI payments. It differs from fraud in that fraudulent intent is not required. Unlike fraud, the intent to wrongfully procure (or increase) benefits need not be established. A "similar fault" determination is made only for the purpose of reopening a prior SSI determination; it is not a criminal matter for which prosecution would be considered.

"Similar" is defined as "nearly corresponding; resembling in many respects; somewhat like; having a general likeness." "Fault" is defined as "an action proceeding from an inexcusable negligence or ignorance that is considered nearly equal to fraud." SSA restricts the definition of fault to "knowledge on the part of the claimant or any other person." The policy is not to penalize a person for ignorance of the law.

"Similar Fault" Criteria

The following factors are needed to establish "similar fault" to reopen an SSI determination which is more than 2 years old.

The changed event is material (i.e., will change the SSI payments) and will create a new overpayment or enlarge an existing overpayment;

A wide discrepancy exists between the new data and the date reported;

"Similar Fault" Definition

The SSI recipient (or other person knowingly completed an incorrect or incomplete report, knowingly concealed events or changes, or knowingly neglected to report events or changes that affect payments;

The event (income, resource, etc.) can and will be verified;

The event (income, resource, etc.) is clearly attributable to the SSI recipient (or the ineligible spouse, parent or sponsor of an alien in deeming situations); and

The case does not involve intent to defraud.

Overpayments

If "similar fault" is detected during SSA development of an overpayment more than 2 years old, SSA can make a "similar fault" determination and reopen the prior determination for the entire period of overpayment (including the period within 2 years).

Where "similar fault" is established during development of an overpayment, the overpaid SSI recipient ordinarily will be found at fault for waiver purposes. However, a third party; e.g., deemor, may be found at fault for reopening purposes, but the recipient found without fault for waiver purposes.

An SSI recipient will be notified when a "similar fault" determination is made. The notice will describe the evidence used to arrive at the similar fault determination. The recipient will receive a notice of any revised determination as a result of the reopening that explains the appropriate appeal rights.

SSA "Similar Fault" Curtailed Development:

In some situations SSA will limit development of "similar fault" because it would be counterproductive; i.e., the effort would exceed any expected results, impose unfair hardships, etc.

A. SSA will not initiate development of "similar fault" in the following situations:

(1) The SSI recipient is dead.

(2) The recipient is 75 or over and is in poor health.

(3) Medical evidence indicates the SSI recipient has an illness expected to result in death in the near future; or

(4) The "similar fault" consists solely of a failure to report a cost-of-living increase in a pension or annuity.

B. SSA will discontinue development of "similar fault" if:

(1) The SSI recipient died after "similar fault" development was initiated;

(2) Reasonable efforts to develop "similar fault" reveal insufficient evidence is available to establish a preponderance of evidence that the event involved in "similar fault" occurred and the excess payment amount is less than the current monthly Federal benefit rate;

(3) Error by SSA employees significantly contributed to the overpayment;

(4) The law or policy has changed so that the event or change would no longer cause excess payments;

(5) The potential excess payment involves a situation difficult to establish; e.g., a number of marital changes, fluctuating living arrangements, exclusive in-kind income, etc.; or

"Similar Fault" Definition

(6) The file contains a favorable determination (initial or appealed) on the issue involved in "similar fault" unless new and material evidence is obtained subsequent to the favorable determination.

Cross References: POMS, sections GN 04070.130 and SM 02001.600 F.8.

Federal Means Tested Benefits

The following programs are the only programs which meet the definition of a Federal means tested public benefit:

- SSI,
- Medicaid,
- Food Stamps, and
- Temporary Assistance for Needy Families (TANF)
- Formerly Aid to Families with Dependent Children (AFDC).

Public Charge

The Immigration and Naturalization Service (INS) is implementing the following definition of "public charge":

"An alien who has become (for deportation purposes) or is likely to become (for admission or adjustment of status purposes) primarily dependent on the government for subsistence, as demonstrated by either the receipt of public cash assistance for income maintenance or institutionalization for long-term care at government expense."

Not all publicly funded benefits are considered in deciding whether someone is or is likely to become a public charge.

Benefits that are considered "public cash assistance for income maintenance" are SSI, cash Temporary Assistance for Needy Families, and State/local cash assistance programs. In addition, the costs for institutionalization for long-term care, which may be provided under Medicaid or other programs, may be considered in making public charge determinations.

(Note: Social Security benefits are not considered to be "public cash assistance for income maintenance" under the INS guidance. Thus, the receipt of Social Security and other earned benefits cannot affect an individual's immigration status.)

Policy effect of INS Public Charge Determinations on SSI Benefits.

The INS public charge guidance does not affect eligibility for benefits under SSI. Noncitizens who are currently receiving SSI and whose health and financial conditions cause them to rely on SSI in the future, may be assured that the public charge policy has not changed the social safety net provided by the SSI program for low-income aged, blind, and disabled individuals.

Disadvantaged by Bad or Delayed SS Department Advice

Often claimants are easily misled, confused, or generally unsure of what is required of them when it comes to protecting their rights. Replies to inquiries are not always clear, concise, correct, and timely.

The intent of the relief to be provided in this situation is to ensure that the result to be achieved is that which would have been achieved had the enrollee (SSA representative) been provided correct, complete, and timely information and had acted accordingly.

An individual may inquire about enrolling or disenrolling for coverage in or before an enrollment period open to him or her and is either provided an incorrect reply or given an accurate reply too late to obtain the earliest entitlement or termination date available by SSA representative. In these cases, very little proof or documentary evidence will be available to substantiate or disprove a statement by the claimant. For instance, an indication in the claims folder that a reply, correct and complete, was prepared timely is not absolute proof that the claimant ever received it. Usually, in a district office interview, the individual is made fully aware of both his or her rights and obligations, but barring such a statement from the District Officer, the word of the claimant must be accepted at face value.

Acronyms

COLA	Cost of Living
DHS	Department of Homeland Security
FO	Field Officer
FRA	Full Retirement Age
HHS	Department of Health and Human Services
HI	Hospital Insurance
IEP	Initial Enrollment Period
INS	Immigration and Naturalization Service
IRS	Internal Revenue Services
ITINs	Individual Tax Payer Identification Numbers
LAPR	Legally Admitted Permanent Resident
OASDI	Old Age, Survivors, and Disability Insurance
PRUCOL	Permanently Residing Under Color of Law
QMB	Qualified Medicare Beneficiary
QI	Qualified Individual
QQ	Qualifying Quarters
SSA	Social Security Administration
SLMB	Specified Low-income Medicare Beneficiary
SMI	Supplementary Medical Insurance
SSDI	Social Security Disability Insurance
SSI	Social Security Income
TANF	Temporary Assistance for Needy Families

Appendix: Donate life: Become an Organ and Tissue Donor

Why should I donate?

Nearly 50,000 Americans are waiting for organ transplants while hundreds of thousands more need tissue transplants. Tragically, *many die* each year because the organs or tissue they need are not available. *You can help save lives by becoming an organ and tissue donor.*

Each day, an average of 17 people who are waiting for organs in the United States, die because no organs could be found for them. This means that each year, more than 6,000 people die in the United States waiting for organ transplants.

You as an organ donor can save up to eight lives. One tissue donor can save or improve the quality of life for up to 50 people.

Remember after our death our body will be burned down. Part of us, our organs will continue to live in different body.

Be selfish and be a noble giver at the same time.

What if one day you need a transplant? Will there be donor to save your life?

Appendix: Donate life: Become an Organ and Tissue Donor

What Can I donate?

Many people with illnesses feel that they have nothing to offer. Many of us have donated or received blood.

Organs that can be donated from living donors include: a lung, partial liver or pancreas, or a kidney.

Organs that can be procured from a brain-dead donor include: heart, intestines, kidneys, lungs, liver, and pancreas

The above are procured where **the family has given consent for donation after cardiac death** also known as **DCD**. This is where the donor has not progressed to brain death.

The following tissues can be procured after brain death (actual death): bones, tendons, corneas, heart valves, femoral veins, great saphenous veins, small saphenous veins, pericardium, skin, the sclera (the tough, white outer coating surrounding the eye).

Is it religiously right to do?

Most of the world's religions support donation as a charitable act of great benefit to the community. Issues surrounding patient autonomy, living wills, and guardianship make it nearly *impossible for involuntary organ donation (Organ Stealing)* to occur.

Hinduism has no opposition to this act of kindness.

Appendix: Donate life: Become an Organ and Tissue Donor

What do I do now?

* Fill out organ donation instruction on back of your driver's License.

* Also fill out an Organ/Tissue donor card. **I have provided some for your convenience on the next page.** Use one and ask you family and friends to use others.

* Tell your family why you feel good about deciding to become a donor.

Your organs and tissue **will not be** donated unless a family member gives consent at the time of your death, even if you've signed your driver's license or a donor card. It's important that you make your family a part of your decision. Tell them about organ and tissue donation and why you feel good about deciding to become a donor. Explain to your family the difference that one person can make. Sharing your decision with your family ahead of time will make it easier for them to carry out your wishes later.

Help Create a Donation-Friendly America!

CALL TO ACTION: You have the power to save lives, to make a decision that will make a difference.

For more information: www.organdonor.gov, www.mayoclinic.com/health/organ-donation/FL00077

Organ/Tissue Donor Card

I wish to donate my organs and tissues. I wish to give:

☐ any needed organs and tissues
☐ only the following organs and tissues:

Donor
Signature _____ Date _____
Witness _____
Witness _____

Organ/Tissue Donor Card

I wish to donate my organs and tissues. I wish to give:

☐ any needed organs and tissues
☐ only the following organs and tissues:

Donor
Signature _____ Date _____
Witness _____
Witness _____

Organ/Tissue Donor Card

I wish to donate my organs and tissues. I wish to give:

☐ any needed organs and tissues
☐ only the following organs and tissues:

Donor
Signature _____ Date _____
Witness _____
Witness _____

Telephone Numbers: California Office: **562-403-1646**
Illinois Office: **847-357-1600**
India Office: **91-097-26575977**